Meet Your
INSIDE
TEAM

HOW TO TURN **INTERNAL CONFLICT** INTO **CLARITY** AND MOVE FORWARD WITH YOUR LIFE

MASTER COACH, CYNTHIA LOY DARST

MEET YOUR INSIDE TEAM

How to Turn Internal Conflict into Clarity
and Move Forward with Your Life

MASTER COACH, CYNTHIA LOY DARST

PUBLISHED BY: TEAM DARST

www.TeamDarst.com

ISBN: 978-0692155196

Copyright © 2018 by Cynthia Loy Darst. All rights reserved. No part of this publication may be reproduced, distributed, or transmitted in any form or by any means, including photocopying, recording, or other electronic or mechanical methods, without the prior written permission of the publisher, except in the case of brief quotations embodied in critical reviews and certain other noncommercial uses permitted by copyright law. For further info, please contact the author at: cynthia@teamdarst.com

PRAISE FOR THE INSIDE TEAM

"Cynthia Loy Darst has written a comprehensive, practical, and highly engaging book to help us all with those pesky (and helpful) voices in our heads. Not only great for coaches, but an amazing resource for anyone who wants to understand themselves better and have practical tools and ideas to help them move from chaos into peace."

ANN BETZ, PCC, CPCC
Director of Research and Learning, *BEabove Leadership*

"The Inside Team has literally changed my life! It's also transformed the coaching work I do with my clients. If you want a truly effective way to break out of stuck patterns and rewire negative habits in your life, then you need to read this book. In fact, get several copies, 'cause you're definitely going to want to pass this along to the people you love."

MICHAEL WARDEN
Leadership Coach and Author

"As my very first coach ever, Cynthia's insightful wisdom changed my life—LITERALLY! She has now taken all that wisdom and framed it into a brilliant, powerful, and awakening book. If you truly desire to understand the ins and outs of how to move forward in your life, Meet Your Inside Team is your doorway in."

RICK TAMLYN
Author of *Play Your Bigger Game: 9 Minutes to Learn, a Lifetime to Live*

"Every once in a while a book is written that has the power to change and elevate lives. Meet Your Inside Team is such a book! At once, this book shines a light on the human condition and shows us how to navigate our consciousness with tools that have a dramatic impact on the way we think, feel, and experience the world. I have purchased copies for my friends, relatives, and colleagues!"

HOWARD VAN ES
President, *Let's Write Books, Inc.*

"Read this if you are ready to take on those sneaky voices in your head that keep trying to make you perfect or safe or look good. Cynthia's concise, humorous look at human nature is brilliant! She'll help you take on one of the scariest things about being a human—meeting internal fear and judgement head on. The exercises in Meet Your Inside Team are liberating—all you need is the courage to try them. And the great part is that this stuff really works! I've had executives, college athletes, and people like you overcome their darkest internal roadblocks as they have taken charge of their Inside Team. You can, too."

SARA SMITH, CPCC, MCC
Executive Coach and Author of *Coach to Coach*

"This book is a practical and delightful roadmap to self-knowledge. Cynthia has combined the best of our Organization and Relationship Systems Coaching (ORSC) model with other approaches as well as her mastery as an individual coach in this book. The Inside Team approach offers an innovative and effective way of bringing systems thinking and team coaching together. Whether you are working with yourself *or coaching an individual, you may think you are working with one person—when in fact, as you will see, you are working with a team!"*

MARITA FRIDJHON AND FAITH FULLER
Founders of CRR Global and ORSC Coaching
Co-Authors of *Creating Intelligent Teams: Leading with Relationship Systems Intelligence*

"I've been a coach since 1994, and if I've learned anything about humans, it's that we are complex, often contradictory creatures. Most of our goals and dreams, as well as our fears and worries, are not cut and dry; they deserve to be respected in a multi-faceted way. Finally, Darst's book comes along and offers an easy-to-use method for communicating with ourselves and our clients that is both accurate and masterful. Thank you, thank you, thank you!"

JEFF JACOBSON, CPCC
Author of the young adult novel *The Boy Who Couldn't Fly Straight*

FOREWORD

Cynthia Loy Darst first came into our lives in 1992. We had just launched our new business, The Coaches Training Institute (CTI), and were in desperate need of people to lead our blossoming roster of courses. Henry had met Cynthia in New York some years earlier where they were both training to be professional actors; he knew that she was a talented live wire and a natural fit as coach and faculty member. So, we invited her to come to the Bay Area and attend one of our original courses. Cynthia fell in love with coaching and together over the next twenty-five years, we grew CTI into the largest coach training program in the world with programs in over twenty countries.

The professional coaching industry was in its infancy back then and no one really knew what coaching was, let alone how to do it. If you said you were a professional coach, people expected you to demand they run laps or drop to the ground and give you fifty. The ensuing years were quite an adventure, filled with the inevitable highs and lows of growing a business in an uncharted industry. Through it all, Cynthia has been a steadfast colleague. She is a potent blend of passion, wisdom, creativity, and heart and we are forever grateful for her guidance and partnership.

We also all share a background in the theater. Though training to be an actor may seem frivolous to some, it's actually an excellent foundation for almost any endeavor having to do with people because it provides a context for deeply understanding the human experience. Each of us is a fascinating constellation of many different facets. We are so alike in many ways, yet so different in others and ultimately complex and often mysterious. Our background in theater has been one of the many rivers that has fed our Co-Active philosophy at CTI. This background has added additional depth to Cynthia's work as well.

We all have many different voices banging around inside our heads and sometimes it can feel like they are in dramatic conflict with each other, pulling us this way and that and keeping us in a cloud of confusion and unease. It can be difficult to sort it all out as we struggle to prioritize the warring voices of our internal dialogue and figure out which one to follow. It can feel a bit like getting a puppy to sit. "Sit! No, no. Sit! SIT!!!"

Meet Your Inside Team offers a restorative approach. What if all of those voices were useful? What if they all had something important to say? What if all the different aspects of us were valuable and worthy of our respect?

Cynthia has a talent for making complex ideas and concepts easily accessible and *Meet Your Inside Team* is no exception. There are several books that teach us how to silence or banish our negative inner voices forever so that we can achieve success. *Meet Your Inside Team*, however, is unique as it shows us how to respect and listen deeply to all of our internal voices so that we can harvest and use their underlying wisdom. It is a book about listening and it is a book about loving and valuing the whole of ourselves, without parsing our parts into "good" and "bad."

Written in an easy-to-read, conversational tone, *Meet Your Inside Team* provides practical models and exercises to support the reader in working with their internal voices. We found the entire book delightful, but our favorite chapter was Chapter Six: Bullies and Gangs—it had us laughing out loud with delight as we immediately recognized our own Bullies and Gangs.

Ultimately, *Meet Your Inside Team* is a book about wholeness as it teaches us how to approach all of wonderful human complexity with respect, curiosity, and love. Sometimes working with our own development can feel very difficult and dark. It's easy to become discouraged and a little hopeless. It is refreshing to have a book that addresses the complexity of our human experience with such playfulness, joy, and heart.

We live in a complex time, full of uncertainty, volatility, chaos, and ambiguity. It's pretty easy to get overwhelmed and feel like the only thing to do is to crawl back into bed and pull the covers over our heads. We very much need models and tools that ground and fortify us and that empower us to approach ourselves and our world with positivity and hope. *Meet Your Inside Team* is such a book. Read it, and more importantly, use it. Working with the questions provided will generate internal harmony and light that can then be reflected externally. In this time of challenge, that light is so needed and we are very honored to be asked to write the foreword for this beautiful book.

HENRY AND KAREN KIMSEY-HOUSE

CO-FOUNDERS, THE COACHES TRAINING INSTITUTE
ASHLAND, OREGON

CONTENTS

INTRODUCTION 19

HOW TO USE THIS BOOK 23

TIPS AND TRAPS FOR COACHES 25

CHAPTER 1   29
WHAT IS AN INSIDE TEAM?

We All Talk to Ourselves, so Who is Doing the Talking? 29

Every Great Team Needs a Leader 33

CHAPTER 2   35
MEET YOUR INSIDE TEAM

EXERCISE 1: QUESTIONS TO HELP YOU DISCOVER YOUR INSIDE TEAM 36

Do I Have Just One Inside Team or Are There More? 37

Context of the Inside Team Approach 39

✏️ EXERCISE 2: SLOW DOWN AND SEPARATE 40

✏️ EXERCISE 3: SPOT THE PLAYERS 42

✏️ EXERCISE 4: MEET YOUR INSIDE TEAM 47

Common Types of Players 48

✏️ EXERCISE 5: NAMING YOUR PLAYERS 49

Not all Players Talk 50

Savannah and the Guard Bunny 52

CHAPTER 3   55
DISCOVER THE WAY THE GAME IS BEING PLAYED

Watching the Interaction and Energy 56

✏️ EXERCISE 6: TEAM DYNAMIC 59

Revealing the System to Itself 60

CHAPTER 4   63
EMPOWERING YOU

Players on Auto-Pilot Who Claim to be You 65

✏️ EXERCISE 7: DISCOVERING YOU	66

CHAPTER 5 69
TRIGGERS, HIJACKS, AND HOW TO RESTORE AUTHORITY

Triggers and Hijackings	69
Soccer and the Psych-Out Kid	72
Hair-Trigger Harry	73
✏️ EXERCISE 8: WHAT TRIGGERS YOU?	73
Hijacking	74
Who Hijacks You?	76
Sharon Meets Stealth Pointer	77
Restoring Authority	80
✏️ EXERCISE 9: RESTORING AUTHORITY	80
Julie Restores Her Authority with Fire Fighter	82
You Can't Erase Your Players	85
People-Pleasing Pete and the Unconscious Agreement	86
Hijacked By Billy the Kid	89

Trapped in the Blanket — 93

Bullying or Conscious Choice? — 94

Safe Sex — 95

CHAPTER 6 — 97
BULLIES AND GANGS

How To Work with an Inside Team Bully — 99

Hijacking Gangs — 101

When a Team Becomes a Gang — 103

The Gotta-Do Gang — 104

CHAPTER 7 — 105
BRINGING IN ALLIES

Taking a Tip from Baseball's Best — 107

CHAPTER 8 — 109
CREATING A NEW PLAYBOOK

Who is in Charge? — 109

✎ EXERCISE 10: DESIGNING THE NEW PLAYBOOK — 110

Running the New Play	*112*
Julie Puts it All Together	*113*
Ben's Boardroom	*115*

CHAPTER 9 — 117
MOVING FORWARD

*****

EXERCISES

EXERCISE 1: QUESTIONS TO HELP YOU DISCOVER YOUR INSIDE TEAM	*121*
EXERCISE 2: IDENTIFY THE PLAYERS	*122*
EXERCISE 3: SPOT THE PLAYERS	*123*
EXERCISE 4: MEET YOUR INSIDE TEAM	*126*
EXERCISE 5: NAMING YOUR PLAYERS	*127*
EXERCISE 6: TEAM DYNAMIC	*128*
EXERCISE 7: DISCOVERING YOU	*129*

EXERCISE 8: WHAT TRIGGERS YOU?   *130*

EXERCISE 9: RESTORING AUTHORITY   *131*

EXERCISE 10: DESIGNING THE NEW PLAYBOOK   *133*

✶✶✶✶✶

WHAT MAKES THE INSIDE TEAM METHODOLOGY UNIQUE?   135

HOW THE INSIDE TEAM WAS CREATED   137

ACKNOWLEDGEMENTS   139

For the One Who Insisted …

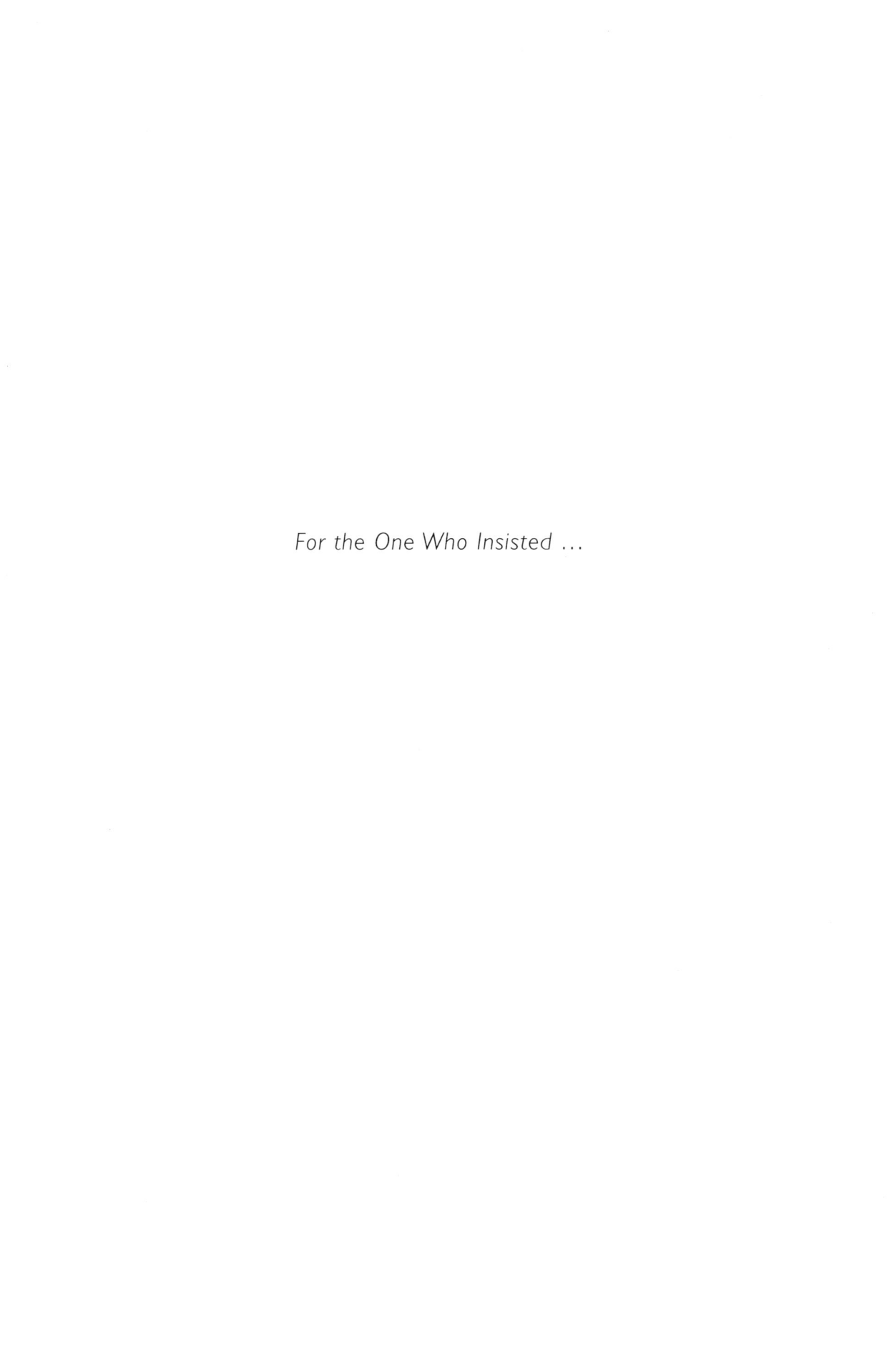

INTRODUCTION

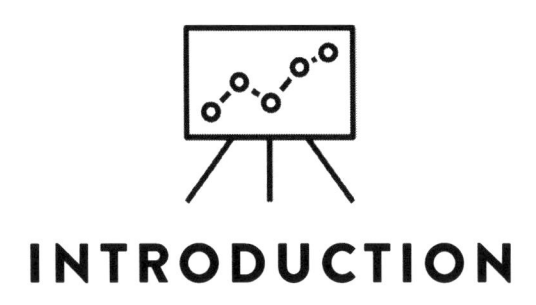

I believe that every human being has the right to fully know themselves, to bring curiosity and awareness to how they think and feel, to have more conscious choice and therefore more power and freedom in the way that they live their life.

For over twenty-five years, I have worked with people as a professional coach. I have seen time and time again how we confuse ourselves, judge and bully ourselves, slug through challenging situations "sucking it up," or use willpower to shut up or ignore the voices in our heads. Everything, that is, but become curious about it and willing to find out what the heck those loud voices are trying so hard to do.

When we stop to think about it, getting louder is a normal human reaction: if someone cannot hear us, we speak louder. And if they still aren't hearing us or paying attention, well, we get LOUDER still!

What if, instead of squelching these loud voices, we find the way to turn toward them with curiosity and respect, turn down the volume, and find out what they're trying to say?

Most of us go through our lives reacting to situations, events, circumstances, and the things that other people do and say. We don't notice that we have gone on autopilot and given up on making conscious choices about how we want to respond to these situations or how we want to live our lives.

I spent most of my formative and young adult years desperately trying to "do it right," never thinking that I was enough. Not good enough, not smart enough, not thin enough, not pretty enough … you name it. Not enough.

Oh, plenty of people in my life tried to convince me otherwise, but it didn't matter.

I had given full permission to a judging bully in my head to collect evidence that I was not enough, and he was doing a damn fine job of it. Every time that he found something new, he would shove it in my face. He made me think that all of that "evidence" was real—was the truth. It was a pretty painful way to go through life.

It wasn't until I was able to notice the conversation in my own head and learn how to become curious about it (thank God for the coaches who have worked with me over the years and pointed me in this direction) that I was able to start having some freedom. You see, most of us think our thoughts are true. We have been listening to the same radio station in our heads for years, and we unwittingly start to believe that it's the only one. Sometimes it's been playing so long that we don't even realize that it's on.

The Inside Team approach gives you a way to go behind the scenes, behind the curtain, so that you can investigate and illuminate the way you think and the thoughts that you believe. By doing that, you will start to unveil the bigger picture of yourself and the many parts of you that make you, well, you. Your creativity and resourcefulness will have room to grow and you will naturally move forward with more ease and clarity.

Einstein said, "Life is too important to be taken seriously." With that in mind, I invite you to a compassionate, respectful, often humorous exploration of how you operate and the many, many parts of you that have gifts to offer.

The Inside Team approach was born of about forty years of personal growth and self-discovery and about thirty years of training and practice with the way that we humans work and think. Look to the Acknowledgements section in the back for a full picture of the many influences that have helped to create this work.

Do you want a greater sense of your personal power? Would you like more freedom and fun? Do you want more clarity and peace of mind? How about less anxiety, less confusion, and fewer negative thoughts? Have I got a treat for you!

HOW TO USE THIS BOOK

The ideas in this book build on each other so I recommend that you start at the beginning. Whether or not you want to do the exercises along the way is up to you. However, if you want to get the most from the book, engaging in the exercises will be the way to do it.

I've illustrated this book with stories along the way. Of course, the names and circumstances have been altered to hold the anonymity of the people involved.

One of the great things about the Inside Team is that once you have the ideas, you will be able to use them in any order that works for you. Something will pop out in a conversation with a friend that is directly from Chapter Four. Maybe Chapter Seven will be your ally today. This isn't a step-by-step process, it's a toolbox to help you get in touch with all the different parts of yourself.

All of the exercises have been collected for you in the back of the book so that it will be easy for you to return to them at any time.

If you want greater understanding of any Inside Team concept, go to: www.TeamDarst.com/InsideTeam. I have some videos for you there.

TIPS AND TRAPS FOR COACHES

If you are already a trained professional coach, you are going to enjoy using ideas from *Meet Your Inside Team* with your clients. Most coaches report that this gives them new ways to address something that they have been hearing from their clients all along.

It's not unusual for a client to come to a session overwhelmed, confused, or feeling stuck. When that happens, listen deeply and pay attention to what they say and how they say it. Chances are that you will hear a conversation that is happening in their head. Let yourself set their topic aside and focus in on the conversation. Introduce this idea of an Inside Team and help them to meet their Players.

This work is somewhat paradoxical as a coach. On the one hand it requires you to be directive while on the other hand you get to hold a lot of space and have the client lead their own exploration.

The directive part is introducing the idea of The Inside Team, setting context for what you want them to do and why you think it might be useful, and then guiding them through an exploration using the questions that you find in this book.

Once the client gets the idea, you get to relax and partner them in their journey. It's easy to get over-excited and start doing the work for them. Instead, it is important that you keep letting go of your ideas and follow their lead.

Check out the videos at: www.TeamDarst.com/InsideTeam where I talk more fully about the Seven Practices of the Inside Team. Info about upcoming Inside Team Coaching Training is also available there.

MEET YOUR INSIDE TEAM

CHAPTER 1

WHAT IS AN INSIDE TEAM?

WE ALL TALK TO OURSELVES, SO WHO IS DOING THE TALKING?

We all have conversations with ourselves. It's not crazy. It's normal; it's how we get through life. We think all day long, and we "hear" our thoughts as voices. Our inner voices tell us what we can and can't, should and shouldn't, must and mustn't do. We have voices that keep us on track or try to derail us, voices that cheer us on or beat us up. Some voices light a fire under our asses, others keep us stuck in the same spot for years. These voices are different parts of us. You know the voices I'm talking about. There's a part of you who wants to spend time with your friends and a part of you that wants to stay home. That kind of thing.

CHAPTER 1

The dialogue from these voices is pretty consistent. They tend to say the same things day after day, especially when it comes to trying something new, putting yourself out on a limb, or taking an emotional risk—whether it's with a significant other, a friend or colleague, or a boss.

If you're like me, your voices are so familiar that you often don't stop to notice what they're really saying and how they affect your daily life and choices.

You might even have a dialogue or conversation going on right now. One voice might be telling you, "this book sounds weird," while another says, "I'm interested; I wonder where she's going with this." In a conversation like that, which voice wins? Do they just keep talking over each other all the time? Do you notice what they're saying? Or does one just silently give in?

Often when this happens, we're so tired of the arguing or the screaming in our heads, the feelings of unrest and inner conflict, that we just avoid whatever it is that's creating these conversations. We stick with what we know, despite the fact that it doesn't make us feel happy, challenged, or fulfilled. We give up on new ideas too early just because they don't feel like the safest option.

Here's an example: Julie was tired of being an assistant in a payroll department. Actually, worse than tired. She felt like a robot—a very grumpy robot. She woke up each morning, stared into her closet, pulled out her clothes, made her coffee, drove to work. She typed her e-mails, handled her tasks, and came home, counting the days until the weekend. She desperately wanted to try something different. She'd always been interested in speech pathology, but any time she began to entertain the idea of becoming a speech therapist, she stopped.

WHAT IS AN INSIDE TEAM?

This is what would happen in Julie's head: The idea of going back to school would start to simmer. She would get excited at the prospect of helping other people, and then …

Voice A: *This could be amazing. I've been thinking about it for ages. It's time to go for it!*

But then …

Voice B: *Are you insane? You can't leave your job, let alone leave your job **and** go back to school! You'll be in so much debt—how will you survive? It'll be years before you can make a living as a speech therapist.*

Voice C: *Plus, what makes you think you could really help anybody? You don't know anything about speech therapy.*

Voice D: *Stop whining about your job! Do you know how lucky you are to have stable work where you make good money?*

Voice A: *But I'm really unhappy there. It's time for me to be happy. Besides, I just want to look into it …*

Voice B: *And have your hopes crushed again?*

Voice E: *Hey, wait a minute. When you've taken on something new in your life, you've always made it work. You could do this!*

Julie spent hours of her life in this crazy-making loop. She didn't need anyone else to tell her that her idea was bad. She was doing it all by herself! Julie hated this conversation. Every time she thought about making a life change, it would start up again and she'd feel horrible afterward. She felt so hopeless and defeated, it seemed like a relief to go back to her old job and numb everything out again.

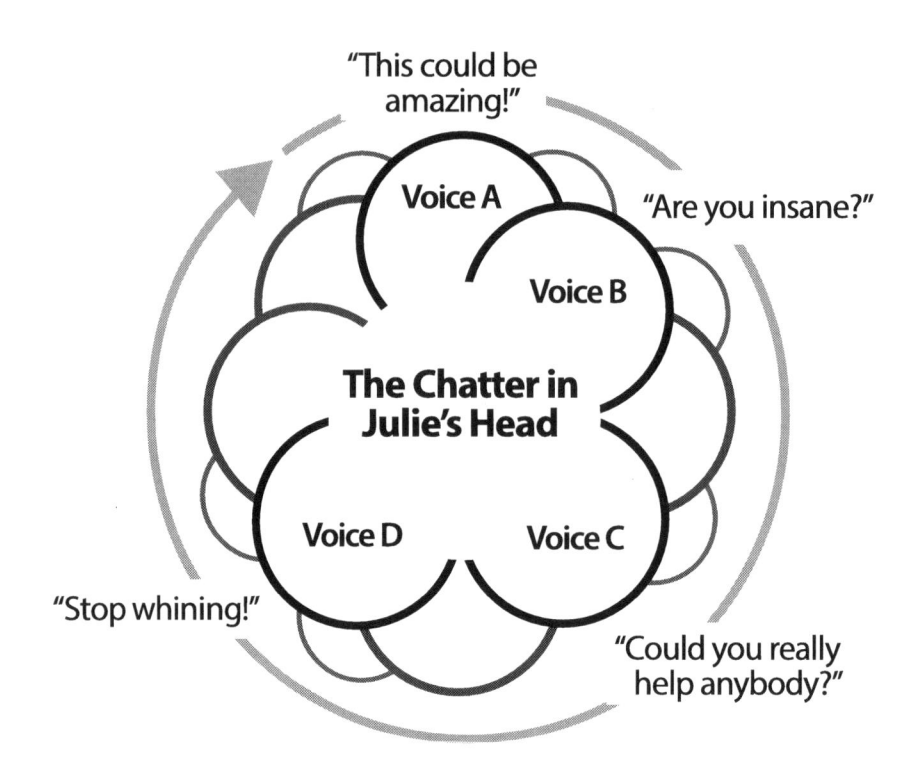

CHAPTER 1

The Chatter in Julie's Head

- Voice A — "This could be amazing!"
- Voice B — "Are you insane?"
- Voice C — "Could you really help anybody?"
- Voice D — "Stop whining!"

We've all been in Julie's shoes. We all know the frustration of trying to overcome a long-standing obstacle or make a significant change in our lives only to find our good intentions derailed by invisible roadblocks that send us careening into a ditch. And here's a thought: while some of these obstacles may be external, most of what gets in the way of our good intentions comes from inside ourselves. Only by going inside can we free ourselves up to move forward toward meaningful action that produces lasting results.

That's where The Inside Team comes in.

The Inside Team is that internal collection of voices, beliefs, and aspects of our personalities that sometimes works in harmony and sometimes doesn't. ***Your*** Inside Team is that collection of voices chattering away inside you. When they argue without resolution, they can limit your effectiveness and stand in your way.

EVERY GREAT TEAM NEEDS A LEADER

These voices, we're going to call them our Inside Team "Players," need a leader, someone coaching the team. In this book we're going to show you how to lead. We're going to teach you a simple, step-by-step method for winning the respect of your Inside Team and using their combined power to create your best outcome every day.

Think of a time you felt amazing. Things were going your way. You didn't notice a conversation between your ears; you just felt **good**. And then something happened. A relationship ended, a work presentation flopped, you were late for your kid's chorus concert—and the inner tumult began.

But what if you became aware of these thoughts? What if you got to know them and prepare for them? What might happen if you actually talked to these voices and figured out what each was saying? What if their contributions had value for you?

When there's awareness and consciousness about these different players in our head then we can work to change our relationship with them. If we don't have awareness, then we cannot have conscious choice—we can't shift anything. One of the main reasons to do Inside Team work is that it takes us to a place of conscious choice. Instead of feeling like life is happening to us, we are back in the driver's seat, having more clarity and power in how we move forward.

That consciousness is the work of the Inside Team. If Julie decided to look at her Inside Team, she might find that Voice B, who keeps yelling "Hold on to your day job," really just wants to make sure that Julie's always taken care of. This Player can't see past the risk to the bigger fact that Julie is a responsible young woman who would never put herself in serious debt. She's certainly resourceful enough to keep her job for now and go to school at night if only she'd allow herself to start exploring.

This sounds obvious, right? It might be obvious to us, looking from the outside, but not to Julie. We're so enmeshed in these different parts of ourselves that distinguishing one from the other can feel like taking your car apart while the engine's running.

But check it out: much of the time, if you're feeling incapable of something, if you're feeling defeated or overwhelmed or just twisty, underneath it all you've got an Inside Team that's not in sync.

Maybe you're not buying this. "Come on, I don't hear voices! It's just me in here."

Yeah? Then how do you explain the way you acted at your Mom's sixty-fifth birthday when Aunt Mona asked you, "Is there someone special yet, dear?"

Who was that raging lunatic that screamed at poor Aunt Mona and stormed out? And then sat in the car for fifteen minutes, too embarrassed to go back? Was that you? Hell, no, that was a Player! You might be suppressing these Players, but they're there. In fact, the idea that we should be able to control our thoughts is actually a Player, and a very dominating one! Once you honestly acknowledge this cast of characters and find out what they're trying to do for you, then you can move forward.

Let's get started! Let's put you in charge so you're not letting your mother or your third-grade teacher or the kid that bullied you on the playground run your life anymore. Let's discover your Inside Team.

CHAPTER 2

MEET YOUR INSIDE TEAM

There's a reason that Pixar made millions on a movie in 2015 about the different emotions in a child's head and how they argue with each other. Everyone knows there's a team of characters inside their heads. In this book, we're bringing them to life in a different way. We're inviting them to pause and come forward. If you want your Inside Team to work well, you have to get to know the players.

Pick an area of your life where you want to see a change but you can't seem to make it happen. Perhaps you want to ask for a promotion at work but haven't been able to do it. Maybe you need to organize your garage, finish your dissertation, get in better shape, or shift a relationship with someone. Take a few minutes just to sit and think about this thing you've been wanting to do. Now start to notice your own thoughts. If you're like most people, it won't be long before you notice there's a dialogue going on in your mind. Take time to listen to each distinct voice, each point of view, each value and desire being expressed.

The dialogue might sound something like this:

"What if I tried this?"

"YES! That sounds perfect. I want to get right on it."

"I don't have time or energy for that."

"But at least I have to try!"

"Maybe I should just give it up completely. It's never gonna happen."

"Yeah, it will! I just need to research it a little more …"

If you're lucky, that's the bulk of the conversation. If you're like some people, just reading this might make you tremendously anxious. These Players are not used to having you notice them. Some of them may get a little squirrelly when you turn your attention their way.

EXERCISE 1: QUESTIONS TO HELP YOU DISCOVER YOUR INSIDE TEAM

So take a moment now, and listen in. Think about that project you are working on or thing that you want to change. Notice your thoughts, notice the dialogue, notice your concerns, and take some notes.

Here are a few questions to play with:

- What is the topic—the project or thing you are thinking about?

- What is your first thought about it?

- What other thoughts, concerns, or feelings come in next?

- What else?

- Does it seem like there is a conversation going on?

- What feels familiar?

- What are the different thoughts, energies, or points of view?

There is good news *and* bad news: For every issue with which you struggle, every relationship you have, every goal you want to accomplish, there's a corresponding Inside Team. When it's going well, you won't notice them. They're working together in harmony, enjoying the ride. They're in alignment and there's a sense of camaraderie. Each Player is clear about their role and they know how to play that particular game.

However, every now and then something happens that gets an Inside Team going. Two or more of your Players will start to jump in with their opinions, ideas, and concerns, and you'll find yourself in a twist. When your Players are vying for attention, it can feel just like kids fighting in the back seat of the car. As the adult who's driving, all you want is to shut them up or tune them out, but neither tactic works for long. Sooner or later, they'll come back. And this time they will be even *louder.*

DO I HAVE JUST ONE INSIDE TEAM OR ARE THERE MORE?

Just so that we're tracking on the same page, try on the idea that you have a multitude of Inside Teams. Some of your main Players may be on more than one team, while others are team specific.

Virtually every topic in your life is going to bring up a conversation in your head.

Here are some places to look:

- Your sex life

- Physical fitness

- Where you live

- Cleaning your house/office

- The work that you do

- Taking time for yourself

- The people you live with

- What's for dinner?

- Changes that you want to make in your life or career

- People who challenge you

- Politics

- Religion

- Vacation: when to take one and where to go

- The list goes on and on.

As you can see, the topics will range from large to small, from the sublime to the ridiculous.

CONTEXT OF THE INSIDE TEAM APPROACH

A few thoughts for you to consider for this Inside Team concept to really work for you:

- Come from a place of curiosity and respect. In this day and age, there is so much in the world about what people need to fix or change to be a better person. Not with the Inside Team. In this work, we are leaning into the Co-Active Coaching cornerstone: people are naturally creative, resourceful, and whole. When we look at our Inside Team through that lens, we easily see the creativity and resourcefulness of our Inside Team Players and ourselves. Rather than consider ourselves as a problem that needs to be fixed, we can find the wisdom and magic in the way choices have been made—the way our Inside Teams have been working so hard to help us.

- We're not here to ask or answer **why** you are the way you are. That would be a very different kind of exploration, one that might get answered with a good therapist.

- We are not looking to eliminate any of your Players.

CHAPTER 2

> They're not bad, and they're all there for a reason. Each of your Players is a part of **you**, just as deserving of love and respect as you are.

So, if we're not going to put them out of their misery, what are we doing? Our focus here is to first become aware of, and then to rework your relationship with these parts of you, these Inside Team Players. You can create a new relationship that will better serve you so that when a Player pipes up inside your head, you can react in a way that moves you forward instead of spinning you in circles.

From the Inside Team perspective, all of your Players have a useful intention. They are on your side, even when they don't seem like it. As you discover your Players, you'll notice that each tends to stand for something that's really important to you. So when a Player tries to take over, it's not about betraying your values. Instead, it's about latching onto one single value and holding it above all others. Staring in one direction all the time, a Player will fail to see the other things that are important to you. And that's where things start to feel off.

The first step toward getting everybody into harmony is to meet the Players on your Inside Team.

✎ EXERCISE 2: SLOW DOWN AND SEPARATE

Think of a topic, maybe one from the list above, or the challenge you worked on earlier in the chapter—the situation you'd like to change but can't seem to budge. Take a few minutes to bring that issue to mind. Tune into the conversation in your head. Notice the thoughts that occur and then start to slow them down.

- There's probably a voice that's quite loud, so let's start with that one. Separate it from the others and bring your awareness to it. What is that voice saying? In what tone?

- You get to use your imagination here: bring this voice out in front of you and imagine it standing there. What does this Player look like?

- Let yourself imagine it like a character.

- What does it look like?

- How does it stand, sit, or move?

- What gestures does it make?

- How is it dressed?

- How old is it?

- What else do you become aware of?

- It has been working hard to get your attention. What is it trying to tell you?

Repeat these steps with any other Players that come up.

As you start to become more aware of these Players, what are you finding out?

As you become aware of the Players, it's important to greet them with curiosity. One thing that keeps the "spin cycle" going is when we think that we already know all about what a Player wants. Just like in everyday life, when we stop listening and stop being curious, it shuts down the relationship.

When you have an Inside Team Player who is constantly shouting at you in a nasty voice, of course you want to shut it up. That makes sense and it's understandable. However, bullying and dominating our Players doesn't work, not in the long run. What we are up to here is creating a conscious and more empowering relationship with all parts of ourselves. That cannot happen when one insists on dominating the others.

It takes practice to come from a curious stance, to listen past what you think the message is—what it has always been—and to listen for the bit of wisdom or truth that is under the nasty energy, even it is only 2 percent true. Learn to listen for the useful information that is underneath the way it is currently being expressed.

EXERCISE 3: SPOT THE PLAYERS

Here's an example from Becky:

"I'm trying to start this new business, and every time I go to work on my website, there's a part of me that says, "You don't know what you're doing!" I've gone to school, I have my degree, and when I work with a client, not only do I enjoy the work; my clients appreciate me as well. But I just **can't get this voice to go away.**"

So far we have two Inside Team Players. Can you spot them? There are two main points of view being expressed.

Player 1 *exclaims: "You don't know what you're doing!"*

Player 2 *defends: "Yes, you do know what you're doing! You're educated you have clients, and you're enjoying your work."*

Dilemma! Conflict! Daytime television in your very own brain! It sounds like these Players are both trying to be right (like there is a right), and if we can figure out which one is right, then it will all be settled! However, that's not the way it works. We need more information. We need to know about these Players and what they're playing for. So here's what we did with Becky:

We had Becky put her Players out in front and start to name them. As she did, we discovered a third one who was saying that she needed to hurry up, that she was behind and taking too long with the website.

We came up with a simple chart that looked something like this:

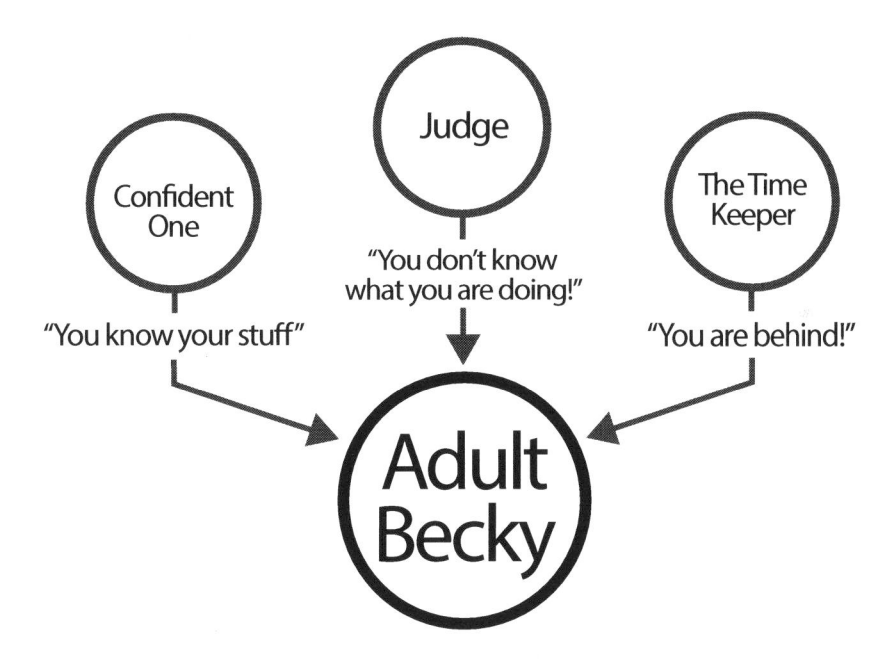

```
        Judge
  Confident           The Time
    One      "You don't know   Keeper
             what you are doing!"
"You know your stuff"              "You are behind!"
              Adult
              Becky
```

Are you starting to get the idea? Now go back to the conversation in your head and begin to chart it out, the way Becky did. You may find you

CHAPTER 2

only have two players to start—or you may find five, six, or seven. No matter how many players you discover this time around, chances are you'll uncover more as we move forward.

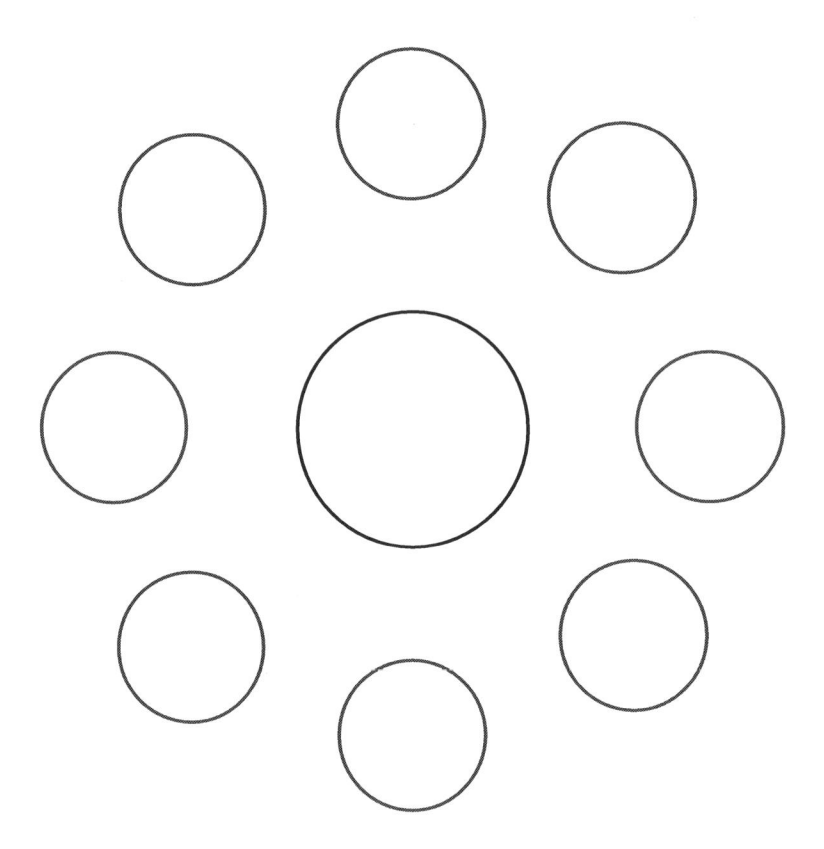

WORKSHEET/DIAGRAM FOR INSIDE TEAMS

Take a look at your diagram. There are bound to be players that you're not crazy about, or even really dislike. Regardless, it's important to hear and honor all your voices. Please, don't ignore a Player just because you wish they weren't there. It's like living with a roommate you hate. You wish they'd disappear, but if you just ignore them your situation will only get worse. Ignoring an Inside

Team Player will never make that Player go away. Instead, the ignored player will get louder than ever. The player may even pop up in other areas of your life where you hadn't noticed them before! Not what we're looking for.

So get really honest about your Players. Know that each Player has wisdom to offer. If you're willing to explore it, you may create a new relationship so different that your feelings for this Player totally change.

If you're struggling to identify the players on your team, don't get discouraged. You're not alone. Most of us, as human beings, don't actually know how to be curious about ourselves. We are so used to our thoughts and beliefs that we don't notice them very often. You're strengthening a new muscle.

You all remember Julie. She wants to become a speech therapist. Voice A agreed and told her it was time to take the leap. Voice B thought she was totally nuts and wondered how she would possibly survive. Voice C was just scared that it wouldn't work out. Voice D wanted her to be grateful for what she had and not rock the boat. Voice E agreed with Voice A, reassuring Julie that she had always succeeded in the past and this time would be no different.

Julie started to really listen to each voice, her Players, and looked at what was going on with each one. She asked herself questions (from the exercises) so she could get to know each of them.

As Julie started really listening to Voice A, she realized that this was her bold, confident self—the one that believed she could explore and go after her goals and dreams. This Player always popped up for Julie. It was the one she really wanted to hear and respond to, even though it often got squashed by all of the other scaredy-cats on Julie's team. She decided to name this Player Joan of Arc.

Voice B was always asking Julie, "Who do you think you are?" —always raining on her parade. This Player knew just how to put her down and even beat her up. As Julie looked at this Player, she recognized that it was constantly putting out any spark of a new idea. She named it Fire Fighter.

Voice C was always saying, "I'm just not sure. I don't know if I can." Voice C was weak, a bit wide-eyed, timid, and overly cautious. Voice C was terrified of making a mistake. She called Voice C Timid Mouse.

In Voice D she found this uptight, pinched-face character that was always saying to her "What about the money? What about the money? What about the money?" Voice D only cared about making sure that Julie was going to be OK financially. That was Voice D's full-time job. She decided to call Voice D Penny Saver.

Voice E was the reassuring one. The one who seemed to know that it would always work out. This reminded Julie of a wise owl and so, that's what she named it: Wise Owl. Here is what Julie's Team looks like now:

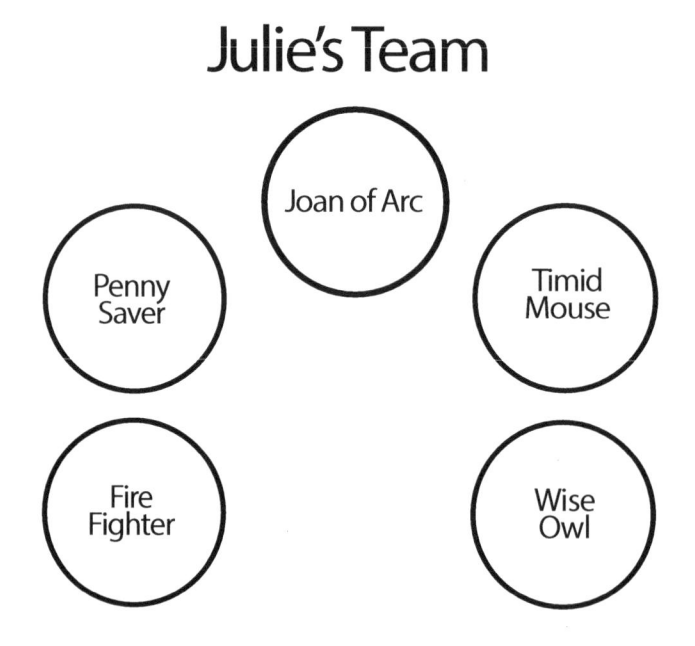

Julie's Team

- Joan of Arc
- Penny Saver
- Timid Mouse
- Fire Fighter
- Wise Owl

See how this works? Let's give it a shot…

✎ EXERCISE 4: MEET YOUR INSIDE TEAM

You are starting to get the idea of the Players. Now it's time to get them out in front of you so that you can see who you have on the team.

Let's imagine that you are putting them out in front of you, perhaps onto a stage.

At this point, let's just bring them out one at a time and find out more about them.

As you answer these questions, you may want to take some notes:

- Which Player wants to come out first?

- What does the Player look like? Stand/sit like?

- What's important to this Player?

- What is it concerned about?

- What does this Player think you are going to forget?

- What does this Player think its job is?

- What job do they want?

- What do they need from you?

- Does the Player have a relationship with or talk to other players on your team or only with you?

CHAPTER 2

COMMON TYPES OF PLAYERS

Following are some archetypes drawn from other subpersonality work. (See the footnotes in the back of the book for more info.)

Quite often Players show up in these roles. This is NOT to name your Players for you, only to offer you some places to look.

Don't feel that you have to come up with a Player for each of these roles: your Players are just as individual as you. If you find yourself asking whether or not a voice is an Inside Team Player, the answer is yes!

- **Protector**: Tries to keep you safe.

- **Judge/Critic:** Hands down verdicts with a nasty or critical energy.

- **Scared Child:** Wants to please everybody and fears any conflict.

- **Champion or Cheerleader:** Urges you on and cheers you up when you're down.

- **Worrier:** Worries. About anything and everything. What if?

- **Ruminator (cousin to Worrier):** Ruminates and re-runs conversations looking for where you messed up and said the wrong thing.

- **Victim:** "This is hard; life is hard. It's not fair." Often feels powerless.

- **Adolescent:** Defies, rebels. "I don't care! Screw you/them!"

- **Creative:** Thinks outside the box. Free; a nonconformist.

- **Overly Permissive Parent:** Lets you get away with things you shouldn't. "More cookies won't hurt; you don't have to do it if you're tired."

- **Nurturing One:** Inner wisdom, reminds you that your health and self-care are essential. (This Player is often missing from the Team.)

- **Wise Elder:** Steps up when you ask. Sometimes known as higher self, future self, or mentor.

Sometimes a Player shows up in a way that is nothing like those listed above. Players don't need to just be characters, either—they may show up as fog, a locked box, a straightjacket, a screen saver, or a ball of flame. Who knows!

✏️ EXERCISE 5: NAMING YOUR PLAYERS

As you start name your players, find names that you relate to, names that will help you personify these players and be able to picture them. For example, I have a player that I call Ms. Train: she's smart, savvy, and impeccably well dressed. She's also a steamroller and quite nasty at times. She will run people over like a train. She is extremely competitive and driven by status.

There are lots of ways to name Players. The one thing that I recommend against is naming a Player an emotion.

For example, lets imagine that there is part of you that feels nervous or afraid.

If we initially call her Nervous Nelly, then she has some room to shift. As you get to know her, she might calm down and then you can call her Nelly. However, if you start by calling her Fear, then she has nowhere to go.

As you get to know your Players they will become more dimensional. Your Fierce Warrior might be pissed and aggressive today, but he won't always be that angry. As you hear him and get to know what he's trying so hard to do, chances are that he will calm down. Oh, he will still be your Fierce Warrior whom you can call on in a moment's notice. He just won't be pissed off all of the time.

It's perfectly fine to call a Player "The One Who _____." The One Who Stands for Truth, The One with the Open Heart, The One Who Plays by the Rules. One of my favorites was The One Who Will Not Be Named.

Let yourself really picture each Player, one at a time. What are their main qualities? How would you describe them? What values of yours are they waving a flag for? Try on a name. You can always change it later if it's not quite right.

NOT ALL PLAYERS TALK

As you look at this list and listen to your team, you may find that there's a Player that's difficult to name or to personify. While some Players are articulate and speak easily, others might just show up as feelings—as though they are pre-verbal. You might find yourself saying something like, "Every time I think of cleaning my garage, I feel so tired," or "There's a weight on my shoulders," or even "It literally feels like a monkey on my back."

This is a Player! In fact, it may be one of the oldest Players on your team, dating back to a time when you couldn't put words to your feelings.

Not all players show up in human form. Instead of a voice telling you something, you might experience a Player as a feeling of anxiety, discomfort, malaise, or entrapment. Maybe it arrives as a sudden weight, making you feel heavy and lethargic. You may try to shake this energy by thinking positively or pushing through it, but it doesn't want to move.

How do you reach out to a Player like this on your Inside Team? Start by choosing a language this Player understands. When I work with clients, I invite them to let go of words and approach this Player physically.

This may feel weird at first, but it can give you powerful results. Here's how it works: Notice where that feeling is. Gently grab it with your hands and pull it away from yourself. Put it in front of you and see what kind of form it takes. In order to do this, you'll want to identify where the feeling lies. Is it sitting on your shoulders? Is it wrapped around your torso? Is it squeezing your head? Find where the feeling exists in your body and physically pull it out in front of you. It might be a big green blob, it might be a straitjacket, it might be a creature or remind you of a character in a movie. It might seem like a blanket, or a thick fog. There are any number of different forms that a feeling can take. You will work with this Player in the exact same way that you work with a Player that looks like a character, creature, or person.

CHAPTER 2

SAVANNAH AND THE GUARD BUNNY

Savannah was a sweet, kind, young woman who had decided to go for a career in acting. When we started our work together, she reported a variety of things she was noticing: she was always exhausted and she was extremely hard on herself. She was also clear that she wanted to become an actress. She was passionate about the work. But she was scared to put herself out there. She was feeling too tired to really pursue work and then she felt bad for not doing all the things necessary in order to really have a career. Negative self-talk is exhausting and she was in a vicious cycle.

As we began to explore her acting career, a specific posture kept coming up—her shoulders came up, her back curled down, slightly hunched, and her hands came up clasping together in front of her chest, sort of like she was holding a basket. We started our exploration with these physical gestures—trying them together, repeating the movements, tuning in to our bodies with awareness. We repeated these movements (shoulders up, hunching forward, hands up) several times, then a string of words came tumbling out of Savannah's mouth: "You don't know what you're doing! You should forget this and go home!"

Once Savannah heard herself say that, she started to laugh. "This Player is trying to protect me, but she feels like a scared little bunny rabbit. Poor thing; she's totally freaked out!" With that, she named this player Guard Bunny.

With a great sigh of relief and compassion, Savannah discovered that she could appreciate Guard Bunny's concerns. "It's true—I don't fully know what I'm doing. I need a plan. But that doesn't mean I need to give up my dream and go home.

When a voice is loud and loaded with emotion, it can feel like (drum roll!) **The Truth**—like we have to do whatever it says. But when we unquestioningly jump into line, we lose conscious choice.

This work is about conscious choice.

Most of us slip into a kind of automatic pilot as we go through life. When we are on automatic we end up making unconscious, life-sucking choices that often leave us feeling obligated, sad, and stuck. By bringing conscious awareness to our Inside Team, to the Players and what they are trying to do for us, we come back to conscious choice. There you can see the bigger picture, work with your Players to create a more empowered relationship with them, and make life-giving choices.

Remember, none of your players are actually bad guys. Each player has something important to say. You might think a Player wants to hurt you or stop you. But sometimes, when a Player keeps screaming, "You don't know how!" it might just be trying to tell you that you don't entirely know how. Here's the good news—if you stop and listen, you might also hear another part of yourself pipe up with, "But I could learn!"

CHAPTER 3

DISCOVER THE WAY THE GAME IS BEING PLAYED

Every Inside Team has a current operating system, a way that their game is played. It's pretty much on automatic. It's not until you slow things down and get curious that you can start to notice how your current system is working. As you begin to listen to each of your Players, you will start to understand the game they're playing.

When an Inside Team is in conflict, there is always a specific dynamic and energetic tone among the players. Most of the time, we're unaware of it. We think it's "just the way it is." But what if I told you that you could take charge and shift that dynamic?

In this chapter, you will come to recognize and explore the unconscious operating system that currently drives the Players of your Inside Team.

CHAPTER 3

WATCHING THE INTERACTION AND ENERGY

Think about the last time you watched a movie or a television show. As an audience member you can see and feel the energy and dynamics of relationships and situations in that show. From your perch on the outside, you can see and understand every action and its consequences. You cringe each time a father pesters his son to be more of a jock. You know he's damaging his child's self-esteem, but you also know he loves his son; he doesn't realize the harm he's doing. You get frustrated when the wife with the huge heart attends to her husband's every need even though he's not thinking about her needs at all. You relate to the drunken sister at the rehearsal dinner who's really just tired of living in her perfect sister's shadow. But you also see the sister who's spent her life never being able to celebrate her own achievements because the whole family was concerned about how her younger sister would react. You are outside all this action, and you get to see the full picture.

We can always assess a situation outside ourselves more easily than one that directly involves us. Think of the last time a friend called you with a problem. You were probably able to help her talk through her dilemma and offer her some new ideas or perspectives. She probably responded, "Why didn't I think of that?" The reason is simple: she was in it. You were outside.

Up until this point, the Players on your Inside Team have been so deeply ingrained in you, it's been impossible for you to see them. But now that you've pulled them out and put them in front of you, you can actually begin to watch how they interact with each other as though you are watching a television show or a movie. You can be outside looking in on all these different relationships.

Besides the Players on your Inside Team, you can also start to notice the interactions and emotional energy between them. Which Players like each other? Who gets excited as we find them? Who is trying to avoid the others? We call this idea: Reading the Emotional Field. This comes to us from the ORSC (Organization and Relationship Systems Coaching) work of CRR Global.

Let's try it with our friend Julie. Every time she thinks about wanting to leave her job or make a shift in her career, the same conversation arises in her head. Her Players argue with each other and Julie gets completely overwhelmed and distraught.

Just let Julie start to think about her dream of becoming a speech therapist, and here they come—Fire Fighter, Penny Saver, and Timid Mouse. They're always ready to gang up on her. Actually, now that Julie has identified these Players, she can see that they're around whenever she contemplates a change of any kind. Penny Saver comes up every time Julie thinks about a financial decision. Fire Fighter is always there to douse that spark when she gets excited by something or someone new. Behind them all is Joan of Arc, who is ready for adventure with guts and gusto. But Joan gets drowned out completely; even when Wise Owl comes to her side, he's not loud enough to carry the day and change Julie's actions. There's some serious conflict here. The voices that are trying to help Julie accomplish her goals aren't even being heard because this Trio of Doom (Fire Fighter, Penny Saver, and Timid Mouse) is so loud. In fact, Fire Fighter doesn't want to let anyone else get a word in. He's running the show, and he's going to keep Julie on track to live a "responsible life" no matter what.

CHAPTER 3

See how that works? The dynamic of Julie's team might look something like this:

```
           Joan of Arc

  Wise
  Owl                    Penny
                         Saver
              Fire
              Fighter
        Timid
        Mouse
```

As you identify the Players on the team, you will start to notice how they work together: who's in charge, who never gets a vote, who tries to contribute but can't get a word in edgewise. Your current operating system, created at an unconscious level, starts to become clear. It is often surprising to discover that you've been letting your tantrum-throwing, hell-raising inner eight-year-old control your finances or your love life. You don't remember putting that little girl in charge!

Listen for which Player (or Players) takes the lead in challenging situations. This can shift from moment to moment. A vulnerable child Player may take over for a moment and then retreat into hiding behind a protector Player who puts out lots of silence, rage, or sarcasm. This powerful protector wants to care of the team, but it may not know when enough is enough.

The Terminator would not be the best person to handle a delicate diplomatic negotiation, yet many of our Inside Teams keep letting our Terminator step in when our inner Gandhi might be better suited to the job.

Start to notice who's the bully, who has a big heart, who is trying to keep you safe, and who keeps stirring the pot. What is each Player's energy? How do they interact with each other and with you? How do they change your thought process? As you start to answer these questions, it may become crystal clear to you why you have been experiencing challenges in making changes in your work or life.

✎ EXERCISE 6: TEAM DYNAMIC

Using your list or the chart you've created for your players, let's start to get a sense of how the team actually operates:

As you asked them to come out in front of you a few moments ago, you may have already gotten a glimpse into this step. Ask your Players once again to come out in front of you. Bring them out one at a time, imagining them out in front of you on a stage:

- Who steps out first? Where does that one go (center stage? Up right?)

- Which one is next?

- And the one after that? (continue to have them come on

to the stage—unless they insist on going somewhere else)

- What starts to happen when they are all there?

- How do these Players interact with each other?

- What patterns consistently arise when you think of your topic or goal?

- Do these players communicate to each other? Or do they only speak directly to you? In either situation, what are they saying or doing?

- Who is standing next to whom?

- Which Players are in conflict with each other?

- Which Player seems to have the most power?

- Who else is here that you have not heard from?

- What else do you notice?

REVEALING THE SYSTEM TO ITSELF

There's not a "right way" for a team to behave. We just want to notice how your team currently interacts. That gives us information about what is working and what is not. When you can see what is happening with your team, you will naturally get new information about how it might operate more effectively. We call this: Revealing the System to Itself. It's another wonderful concept that comes to us from CRR Global (formerly The Center for Right Relationship).

The idea is that when a system can "see itself," it will naturally want to self-correct. It's a bit like when you look in the mirror and notice that you have spinach in your teeth, you will naturally want to remove it.

Some Inside Teams work like a pinball game, fast and wild, with energy and thoughts moving rapidly from one Player to the next. On other teams, the Players hardly interact at all; they just stand there and look at you, like Children of the Corn.

What if you had a team of employees who ignored you and spoke only to each other? Weird, huh? But some Inside Teams are like that when we first tune into them. They are so used to disagreeing with each other and trying to get their voice heard, they have forgotten that you exist.

On the other hand, what if you managed a basketball team where one player refused to pass the ball to his teammates? Imagine, over and over that player just keeps grabbing the ball and ignoring the rest of the team. Good lord! Chances are, that team would lose. It's rather obvious that for a team of any kind to really thrive, cooperation and collaboration between the Players is going to be needed.

Dominant Players love to steamroll the rest of your Inside Team—which means that some of your Players may not even be getting into the game! They might be really smart, but they can't help you if you can't hear them.

Or maybe nobody dominates; everybody's talking and it's total mayhem in there.

It feels like that time your mother called while you were cooking dinner for the kids and your significant other was yelling from the den and the dogs were barking and one kid started tattling on the other and you felt your head explode. Yeah. Boom. Like that.

However chaotic your Inside Team dynamics have been, trust me, there is hope! As soon as you recognize your Inside Team and your Players and see the team dynamic it will start to evolve. Your Inside Team, your internal system, has been revealed to you.

Remember, systems are self-correcting. The simple act of noticing something makes it start to change. So as soon as you recognize your Players, you'll start to see how they interact when you're confronted with a certain situation. And once you see what's going on, your Inside Team may naturally start to correct itself.

CHAPTER 4

EMPOWERING YOU

Now you see all of these different Players—you have Mrs. Doubtfire out in front of you, Darth Vader to the left, Angel Spirit to the right, and Mischief Maker zipping around in circles ... well, who are *you*? Are you one of them? Are they all part of you?

Let's slow this down and take a look. There is someone who can see and hear these Players: someone with the power to pull them out, notice their energies, and hear what they say. That person is you. Many disciplines describe this aspect of your being as the observing self, the adult self, the deep self. We're just going to say You.

The You is the self that is aware of all the other voices and can identify their roles and alliances. The You is a nonjudgmental observer. The You can watch what's happening on your Inside Team without judgment, ego, or attachment. The You is interested in and curious about the wisdom of each Player. If you have a strong reaction to a player or a

CHAPTER 4

point of view, well then, that's not You. It's a stealthy little Player trying to act like You, but it's not the real You.

Wait, what!? How do you know?

Here's how you know: If you find yourself saying, "I can't stand that Player—he's so annoying," then you know you have another Player on your hands, not the real You.

Wait a minute. This is getting confusing. You have all of these Players and you have You—which one is real?

Well, they all are. They are all aspects of you. While there are certain ones whom we relate to and identify most easily with, all of them are real parts of yourself.

In talking with my colleagues and other Inside Team coaches about You, we found that it's easy to go down a rabbit hole with this idea. There are so many thoughts and philosophies about what our core self might be. So for now, let's make this easy. Through the lens of The Inside Team, You is the one who can see the others and comes from a neutral, non-judgmental stance.

And why do we need to get to You?

Because you are the one who can change the way your Inside Team operates. Only you can free yourself of any hold they may have on your current life or goals. So take a few minutes before moving on. Think about Julie in Chapter One, feeling stuck in her work and her desire to live a more fulfilled life. She's been letting some naysayer Players take over whenever the thought of change arises, making change a horrifying thing and keeping her stuck in a place where she's not happy. However, in connecting to her core self (her You), Julie realizes that these guys aren't in charge at all and that she's actually been allowing them to take over and control her actions.

PLAYERS ON AUTO-PILOT WHO CLAIM TO BE YOU

My client Paul reported on one of his Players, one that he calls What Will People Think? He calls him Willy for short.

> *Willy is always so concerned about what other people think. As I start getting to know him, I can see that his concern is there for a good reason. He wants me to be respected and in good relationships with people. He actually cares about people, but the way he's playing his role has me so on edge that other values of mine aren't getting honored. I'm starting to resent the people who I'm trying to look good for of all the time—even though it's not their fault!*

Players like Willy become so engrained in our operating systems that it feels like they're who we are. But they are not your core essence. They've become such a strong part of your identity that you didn't know that you could make any changes to them. But now that you have awareness it's a whole new ballgame. *All of these Players belong to you. You do not belong to them.*

I'm going to say that again*:* **These Players belong to you. You do not belong to them.**

Take that in for a moment.

Until now, you've been letting them run the show. But the truth is, you are in charge. And you carry the ultimate power to determine the course ahead.

More than one "Aha!" has come from situations where some nasty vicious Judge Player has been sniping away, perhaps for years, at someone. And that someone finally realized that they had somehow been letting that Judge run their life for all those years when in fact they were really in charge.

CHAPTER 4

✎ EXERCISE 7: DISCOVERING YOU

By now, the idea of noticing a Player and putting them out in front of you is starting to feel more familiar.

This time, as you do that, pause to notice that there is **someone** who can see the other Players. That is You.

When we were children and we watched movies, we were terrified of the Wicked Witch, the nasty teacher, and the evil characters. We thought that they were going to get us!

As you have grown up, you might still get nervous watching a movie from time to time. However, I assert that generally speaking, you understand that for the story to be compelling there are a variety of roles that need to be occupied. If there is going to be a good guy, there needs to be a bad guy. It makes a story even more interesting when every character has something that they are passionate about, something that they are totally committed to, something that makes them three-dimensional.

Our Inside Teams offer us a rich and wonderful story when we take the time to slow it down, get to know our Players, and stop resisting what they have to offer.

As you rest into the You of you, allow yourself to be curious about and fascinated by your Players. Let yourself explore what is important to them, what they are passionate about, and what they are working so hard to try to get you to see.

In my experience, Players can often come off as nasty, negative, or evil when they don't know how else to get our attention.

As you see the dynamic and the roles that your Inside Team Players have been cast in, you'll also start to see what might work better for your team. When you can get that view of your internal system, you will naturally start to redesign how the game is played.

If it is now obvious to you what to do with your Inside Team, go ahead and skip to Chapter Eight: Creating a New Playbook. However, if something keeps going squirrelly, if one of your Players just keeps running the show, then check out this next chapter.

CHAPTER 5

TRIGGERS, HIJACKINGS, AND HOW TO RESTORE AUTHORITY

"All of the significant battles are waged within the self."
- Sheldon Kopp

You've met your Players, you've discovered the way they interact, and you've found the You in all of this. But hold on—before you design a new game plan for the team, let's talk about a dynamic that happens for all of us from time to time: triggering and hijacking.

TRIGGERS AND HIJACKINGS

There are two different kinds of circumstances where Players take over without your permission. One happens from the outside in. We refer to this as a trigger. The other happens internally; we call this a hijacking. Let's look at examples of both so we can see what happens and how to work with them.

Here is a trigger that many of us have experienced: You're driving down the highway on a gorgeous afternoon. There's a hint of spring in the air. You have your favorite music playing and you're singing along. Out of nowhere, a fast little car cuts in front of you—no signal, no warning, no manners. Instantly your carefree self is out the window. You lay on the horn and scream, "**You jackass!** Where'd you learn to drive?" The fast car has already sped out of sight, but you went from zero to sixty in three seconds, all because some stranger cut you off. Beet red, palms sweating, heart racing—you were triggered!

It's one thing to feel upset by something. However, when the reaction is far greater than how you would want to respond, you're dealing with an Inside Team Player.

Hijacking is more subtle; it comes from within. You've spent years building your business reputation. You've earned promotion after promotion and provided for your family. But you're starting to feel like it's coming at a cost. You're rarely home for dinner anymore. Even on the weekends, your kids expect to see you on a business call in the middle of their baseball game. They've stopped asking if you saw the hit they got or if you'll be able to be at the Spring Concert at school. They just know you won't.

It's not what you want—your definition of being a good father entailed far more than simply providing for them. But it seems that every time you plan to be around, you get derailed. You plan to be home for dinner, but a conference call comes up that you have to be on. You swore you wouldn't work all weekend, but on Friday you get hit with the news that your client needs a project finished days sooner than originally planned. You're almost ready to book a summer vacation, but news comes that there's a conference and your boss has chosen you to attend. It doesn't sound like you're getting hijacked—does it? That's because this hijacking Player, let's call this one King of the Mountain, has planted himself on your shoulder for the past twenty years. He is all about success and status at work. He's whispered in your ear every time you've tried to leave the office a little early, every time you've thought about taking a vacation, every time you've thought about passing along a responsibility to someone else so that you could get to your kid's game. King of the Mountain was there, telling you that if you did any of those things or put your family first, someone else would get that promotion. Someone else would get the raise, someone else would get noticed by the boss. King of the Mountain is all about your success in the workplace, no matter how it affects everyone else around you.

In both of these situations, the lasting effects can ruin your day. And the long-term impact can mess with a lot more than that. Let's look at little more deeply into triggers and hijacks.

A trigger is an event that causes a chain reaction. It pushes the first domino. There are fifty million triggers for people. Your six-year-old child cuts off her bangs all the way to her forehead. Your boss yells at you about the job you're doing. Your flight gets canceled and it blows your schedule. The man you adore comments on how sexy he finds a friend of yours. The people at the next table in a restaurant are just too loud. Your girlfriend complains that you're not paying enough attention to her. You are pushing to meet a deadline at work and your computer crashes. You're accused of something you didn't do. I'm guessing you can relate to at least one of these.

Try on this metaphor: Your day is rolling out more or less according to plan. You feel calm and focused. Suddenly the "trigger" rings your front doorbell, and just as you go to answer it, one of your Players jumps in front of you and answers it first. It goes without saying that the calm, centered, adult You knows how to answer a door and deal with almost any situation. But just as you go to open the door, this Triggered Player jumps in front of You, pushing You aside, and answers and says "Don't worry, I've got this!" and then proceeds to answer that front door in their own way.

When you're triggered, you might yell and scream. You might get nasty, defensive, arrogant, or cold. You might freeze like a deer in the headlights. You might get silly, shy, or giggly. All of these reactions are the impact of a Triggered Player taking over without our permission.

SOCCER AND THE PSYCH-OUT KID

One of our Inside Team coaches was working with a college soccer team. She was getting them in touch the idea of The Inside Team, and they were starting to notice their Players. One of the forwards on the team, Nicole, raised her hand and asked for help. She told us about an opponent on another team who really knew how to push her buttons. The other kid used derogatory comments as a weapon, and Nicole's game was suffering because of it.

In one game, Nicole came extremely close to making a goal. It was a great effort and she barely missed. The opponent came up right next to her and whispered, "Too bad. A little more practice, and you might be good enough to play in this league."

A couple more barely audible comments and Nicole was completely triggered. She got angry in her effort to prove her opponent wrong. Her anger invited desperation—the fear that maybe she actually couldn't play the game. That compromised her ability to think clearly, control her shots, and even stick with the game plan. Naturally, Nicole fell apart, and her team lost.

It was mission accomplished for the young provocateur on the opposing team: she had psyched out her biggest threat.

HAIR-TRIGGER HARRY

Harry was head of sales for a major national company when I started working with him. He was as smart and strategic as they come—a true asset to his company in many ways. Except that he also had a reputation as a hothead, constantly overreacting when someone didn't do something exactly his way. He insulted and demeaned his staff and colleagues rather than talking through challenges and creating more effective ways to work. Harry hated how his temper kept getting the better of him, but he didn't know what to do. When something didn't go as planned something in him just snapped. It was like someone else took over! He didn't want to explode like that—he just did. And he felt helpless to do anything about it.

Fortunately, there was something Harry could to change his behavior. But first he had to understand what was going with his Inside Team and meet the Player who kept taking over. He needed to know his team's current operating system before he could change it.

EXERCISE 8: WHAT TRIGGERS YOU?

Now that you have had a couple of examples, let's turn our attention back to you:

- What kinds of situations trigger you?

- What kinds of people?

- What specifically do they say or do that triggers you?

- How do you know that you are triggered?

- What are your behaviors? Do you freak out? Freeze up? Act superior?

HIJACKING

Now let's look at hijacking. Hijacking works from the inside out. One of your Players steps up with an idea, and you buy into it so quickly that you don't even notice. Hijacking Players like to sit on your shoulder, waiting to take over and steer you in a direction that you'd rather not go. Later, you'll look back and know this didn't feel so great, but you may not actually understand what really occurred.

In our world there's a lot of talk about "having the willpower" to change, to overcome something. But that "willpower" talk, and the judgment that goes with it, tends to miss the point. The real reason we don't change is that the conversation inside our heads has not changed. If you haven't taken the time to really hear your internal conversation, it can be extraordinarily challenging to change it.

Many of us change our conversation by listening to someone else do the talking. We watch TV or listen to friends and family; we pick up a tip from Dr. Oz, Oprah, or Suze Orman. For a few days this new information comes into our thinking, but most of the time it doesn't stick.

If you're anything like me, you've faced a situation like this: You've made a clear decision that you want to eat in a more healthful way, which includes having lots of vegetables and lean proteins every day. You have very consciously decided to forgo desserts for the time being. You come home from work and it's been a killer day. You are tired, hungry, and grumpy. You go to the kitchen and wonder to yourself what you can eat. As you open the cabinet:

Player A: "Gee, look at those cookies!"

Player B: "Wait, you said that you were going to eat healthy."

You: "OK, so what do we have?"

Player B: "Ummm. Carrots?"

You: "Damn, I need to cook. I forgot to go by the store."

Player A: "Cookie?"

You: "No."

Player A: "You can eat healthy later … it's just this once."

Player B: "No, you know better."

Player A: "You're too tired to cook. It's late."

You: "Well…." (sinking feeling.)

Player A: "One cookie won't hurt."

(You pick up the cookie, considering it)

Player A: "It's oatmeal; it's good for you!"

You feel bad, eat the cookie anyway, and spend the rest of the evening beating yourself up about the whole thing.

Sometimes the Hijacking conversation happens even faster than that. Experienced Players are stealthy. They are as wily and strategic as you are. You know you have been hijacked when, at the end of your day, you didn't do what you planned and you're disappointed or upset about it. Maybe you worked late when you meant to get to the gym, perhaps you played games on your iPad when you meant to finish a project, or maybe you intended to spend time with your family but spent the day answering e-mails.

Here's the scoop: There's nothing wrong with doing those things. In fact, spontaneity can be a delight! Getting work done, playing video games, answering e-mails—they're all fine, when you consciously choose them. However, when you've been hijacked, you're doing things without much thought. They seem like a good idea at the time, like they'll just take a minute. Maybe they never even rise to awareness, like when you "wake up" and realize you just ate half a chocolate cake! That's not a conscious choice. Not when you're being hijacked into an action that won't end with the result you want.

WHO HIJACKS YOU?

Think of a situation where you mean to do one thing, but often end up doing another.

Let yourself imagine that situation. Bring it into focus as clearly as possible.

Now, slow it down in your mind, and see if you can notice the Player who hijacks you.

- What do they do?

- How do they do it?

- What is the energy of it?

- What do they say to you? Or have you believe?

- What is the impact on you?

- Who believes what the hijacking Player is telling you?

SHARON MEETS STEALTH POINTER

It took a long time for Sharon to know she was loved. Although she came from a supportive, loving home, Sharon never felt she was really important to anyone. Even when she got into a serious romantic relationship, she never trusted that it was real unless she was actually being shown. When Marco told her that he loved her, when he showed his affection, she felt it. Unfortunately it only lasted for that moment. As soon as that moment was over, she was bursting with insecurities about their relationship.

The next day, Sharon always found herself wondering if Marco still

CHAPTER 5

loved her, if he still wanted to be with her. She noticed all kinds of little signals that Marco didn't care anymore. He would look at other women, check his cell phone while they were together, or watch a TV show instead of having a conversation with her—and she would assume it meant he didn't want to spend time with her.

As time went on, Sharon realized that this was not helping her relationship in any way, shape, or form. Rationally, she knew that Marco loved her, but she couldn't stop the voice that questioned it constantly. As Sharon started to bring this into awareness, she realized that she was experiencing a very sophisticated hijack. This Player was so subtle! She noticed that it felt like he was whispering in her ear and finding evidence at every turn to support Sharon's belief that she wasn't important enough for someone to love her.

Sharon grabbed that energy whispering in her ear and put the Player out in front of her. He was lean and taunt, dressed in black, carrying a sniper rifle. Sharon named him Stealth Pointer because he loved to whisper in Sharon's ear, pointing out each action that seemed to prove Marco didn't care anymore. These insidious little moments were undermining her relationship.

Stealth Pointer was really just trying to protect Sharon. He was making sure she wasn't going to get hurt, that she wasn't being stupid, that she wasn't going to get duped. Stealth Pointer refused to let Sharon look stupid.

When Sharon decided to restore her authority with Stealth Pointer, here's how the conversation went.

Sharon: *"Hey there, slippery one. I feel you whispering in my ear and pointing things out."*

Stealth Pointer: *"Yes! Look over there!"*

Sharon: *"What is it that you are trying to do?"*

Stealth Pointer: *"I'm trying to protect you. I don't want you to be foolish. It's not safe."*

Sharon: *"Thank you. I'm grateful for that. However, the way you're trying to protect me isn't helpful. It's making me feel nervous and anxious."*

Stealth Pointer: *"Well, too bad. I'm keeping you safe."*

Sharon: *"I get that you're trying to keep me safe. But the way you're doing it makes me feel more afraid. It's time for us to shift the way we work together."*

Stealth Pointer looks at Sharon like she's totally lost her mind.

Sharon: *"Rather than feel afraid of people not loving me, I'd like to focus on the ways they do love me. What would you think of pointing out the ways that Marco does love me, rather than the ways he doesn't?"*

Stealth Pointer: *"I don't know. Would that keep you safe? "*

Sharon: *"I think it would. I would certainly feel safer. And, I am an adult now; I can handle it if there is actually a problem."*

Stealth Pointer: *"You can? Oh. What if I just stay at your shoulder?"*

Sharon: *"OK. Let's try this. You stay next to me; I'm going to be watching for the ways that Marco loves me. You can help me with that, and your job* *is also to watch for any real threat to me. Not weird little things that Marco does."*

Stealth Pointer: *"OK, that sounds better. I can do that."*

The simple awareness that Stealth Pointer existed helped Sharon to stop him from running the show. When she was able to look for the ways that Marco showed his love, she realized that Marco did love her—day to day, moment to moment—and she could let go and enjoy their relationship. Meanwhile, Stealth Pointer was still there to let her know if she needed to be careful in a certain part of town or have a heightened awareness of her surroundings.

RESTORING AUTHORITY

In order to move forward, you need to take control again. You need to have the player that's been taking over this part of your life stand down and you need to step up to the plate. You need to take the reins back.

When we work with a Triggered or Hijacking Player it can be very powerful to go through a process called Restoring Authority. It goes like this:

✎ EXERCISE 9: RESTORING AUTHORITY

Notice and Separate

Notice that there is a Player who hijacks you or the one who reacts to the trigger. Usually, you can feel it in your body. Grab on to that energy with your hands and pull it outside of yourself so that you can separate from it and have a conversation.

You might want to work with a partner or a coach to do this—sometimes it can be hard to separate from the Hijacking or Triggered Player.

Describe the Player and Name It
Really personify him or her—what does this Player look like? Sound like? What does their energy feel like? What might you call this Player?

Give Voice to the Player
What is this Player trying to do? What does he/she want? This Player takes over because they have an important and valid concern. What is this hijacking Player so concerned about? What is the wisdom this Player might have for you?

Find the Unconscious Agreement
Some time ago, you might have been a child, this Player appeared when you needed them. He/she helped you out of a tight spot when the younger you didn't know how to deal with the situation. At that moment, you made an agreement. It's probably an agreement that you don't remember making, that's why we call it the unconscious agreement. What is it that you and this Player agreed to? Under what circumstances is he/she supposed to step in and take over?

Facilitate a Conversation with the Player
In this situation, it's common to ignore the Player or even pretend that he/she doesn't exist. Maybe you've hated that part of yourself, so you've tried to get rid of it. Now it's time to acknowledge this Player and ask why they keep trying to take over. If he/she were a close friend or colleague and you needed to work through a conflict

together, what would you say? It's important that your hijacking Player feels fully heard and understood. If they can see that someone else, you or perhaps a different Player, can handle the situation, they might be willing to step down.

Create Clarity

Identify how you want to respond to the situation, instead of having the Player take over.

Create a New Agreement

It's time now to create a new agreement with the Player. While they need to be able to align with it, you need to step into your authority, your adult self, and design the way that you want to respond when that trigger show up again.

Imagine the Trigger (or Hijacking Situation)

Play it out in your mind. How will you enact this new agreement next time this situation occurs?

JULIE RESTORES HER AUTHORITY WITH FIRE FIGHTER

Let's go back to our friend Julie. It's time for her to restore authority on her Inside Team.

Just a reminder, when she started to consider the dynamic of the team (in Chapter Three) it looked like this:

[Diagram: Four circles labeled "Joan of Arc", "Wise Owl", "Penny Saver", "Timid Mouse" surrounding a central circle labeled "Fire Fighter"]

It can work well to start with the loudest Player the one who's been wreaking the most havoc, so she turned her attention to Fire Fighter.

After getting in touch with the Fire Fighter and bringing his energy out in front of her, their conversation went like this:

Julie: *"Fire Fighter, I am* **really** *ready for some change in my life. I'm not happy, and I don't want to spend the rest of my life stuck in a job wondering 'what if.' However, every time I start to look at options, I find you there, telling me to stay put and just be happy with what I've got."*

Fire Fighter: *"Yup, stay put. You're safe here. Stop trying to start something new."*

CHAPTER 5

Julie: "What are so concerned about?"

Fire: "Concerned? I'm concerned that you won't be able to handle the disappointments. I'm worried that you'll fall apart if things don't go like you plan. It's safer to just stay the same."

Julie: "So are you trying to keep me from getting hurt? From having any disappointments or failures? That's what it sounds like."

Fire: "That's **exactly** what I'm trying to do!"

Julie: "So it sounds like, a long time ago, we made an agreement that any time I thought about stepping outside the box or taking a risk, you would stop me in order to keep me safe. Is that right?"

Fire: "**Yes!** If you take risks, you might fail, and what will happen then? We'll be out of control!"

Julie: "I really appreciate what you've been trying to do. However, I'm an adult now and I can handle the bumps in the road. Stopping me from trying things that excite me—things I'm really curious about—is hurting me more than the failure I might suffer if I try. I know there's a chance it might not work out, but guess what? There's just as big of a chance that I could succeed and be happier than I've ever been. And I really feel ready to take those risks and find out. That feels better than just sitting around and staying unhappy."

Fire: "Hmmm. If I'm not keeping you safe, then what do I do?"

Julie: "Well, I don't want you to go away. I want you to stop squelching ideas before they even start. What if you stay nearby and help me to *watch ideas as they grow. It will be like watching a spark become a fire—a controlled fire. We want it to burn in the fire pit and grow in a safe way, but not jump into the field and burn out of control."*

Fire *(finally relaxing)***:** *"I could do that."*

Julie: *"OK—so now let's think about me going back to school. Let's imagine me starting to explore a new career. I want you with me on this adventure. You'll be my wingman. If you've got my back, then I can look a few steps forward and we can get some new ideas going."*

Fire: *"Hum. Well, OK, let's try it."*

That is how Julie restored her authority.

Notice what Julie did: She had to first notice which Player was taking over without her permission. Once she found Fire Fighter, she started a conversation with him, finding out what he was trying to do for her and what he was so concerned about. It is normal for Players to think that you are still a child and that you cannot take care of yourself. Until you draw attention to the fact that you are a grown-up they usually aren't willing to change.

YOU CAN'T ERASE YOUR PLAYERS

Notice how quickly you want to control a Player or just get rid of it. I know: you have willpower. You think you can. But I promise you, if you don't actually work **with** this part of you to create a new relationship, it will continue. It will get louder and more creative in its ways to get through to you. Some Players are like that concoction you made in fifth grade. You weren't supposed to put a lid on it, but you did—and the next day, boom! It exploded all over your bedroom.

Many of us are ashamed of these different parts of ourselves. You think, "I can't believe I have this part that's so eager to be recognized" or "I can't believe this part of me is so rude to people." Or you think, "I'm a strong, confident woman. Why should I feel like a victim?" Or "I can't believe I'm worried that no one will ever love me."

This is not about judging or shaming ourselves for these different parts. Eliminating these Players would not make you better off. What we want is to bring curiosity, compassion, and awareness so that we can find out what each Player is actually trying to do. They all serve a purpose, and every one can benefit you once you shift the relationship that you have with them.

PEOPLE-PLEASING PETE AND THE UNCONSCIOUS AGREEMENT

You had a teacher who was a screamer. You got caught whispering; she screamed. You dropped your pencil on the floor; she screamed. She waited for you to screw up so she could scream. You hated getting screamed at, and you were too young to know how to handle the situation, so a part of you stepped up as protector. We'll call this Player People-Pleasing Pete. Initially, he interacted only with that specific teacher. But before long, Pete was looking for any opportunity to protect you. Any new teacher, any new authority figure, triggered Pete. He told you to be invisible, stopped you from asking questions, and made you say yes to whatever the teacher asked—no matter what. Now People-Pleasing Pete is so much a part of your identity that he's totally on automatic. When a friend calls and asks if you can pick up the cake for the party this weekend, even though you have absolutely no time, Pete jumps in and says, "Sure!"

People-Pleasing Pete wants everyone happy, with every need met. He's in clean jeans and a collared shirt so that he looks nice but won't stand out from the crowd. He doesn't see what **you** need, because it's more important to keep things comfortable for everyone else. It's hard for him to let on when something upsets him. In fact, he'd rather just take one for the team than allow you to mention that you might want something different. He's afraid to rock the boat. He wants everyone to like you all the time because he wants your relationships to feel good.

Once you've discovered Pete and put his energy outside of you, a conversation to restore your authority might go something like this:

You: *"Pete, I feel like I'm always putting everyone else first, and in doing that, I'm not taking care of myself. I know you want what's best for me."*

(As you say this out loud, how's Pete responding? We want to hear from him. That's how you get into a better relationship. It needs to be a conversation.)

Pete: *"But you have really good friends, and I don't want you to lose them! What happens if someone gets upset with you? What if they stop inviting you to do things? What if you end up alone?"*

This part of you (Pete) may think you're still a child; he doesn't realize that you are now capable of handling this situation differently. It seems you made an unconscious agreement with this part of yourself, probably many years ago, that when a situation with other people arises, Pete steps up to the plate.

CHAPTER 5

You: *"So what are you worried about, Pete?"*

Pete: *"I'm concerned you're going to say something rude. I'm concerned you're going to be inconsiderate."*

You: *"So what are you trying to protect me from?"*

Pete: *"I don't want anyone to yell at you. Or worse, to stop being your friend."*

You: *"Apparently, we made some kind of agreement a long time ago about how you would step in to take care of things. What's that agreement?"*

Pete: *"We agreed that I would stop you from upsetting anyone who's important to you. We agreed that I wouldn't let you rock the boat. I'm trying to protect you."*

You: *"Wow. You've been working so hard. Thank you! However, now that I'm an adult, it's important for me to take care of myself first. I end up feeling angry and resentful when I don't. I also believe my relationships are more authentic and honest that way. It's time for me to notice what I want and speak up about my needs, as well as considering others'."*

Pete: *"I'm not so sure about this. How are you gonna pull it off?"*

You: *"I've got skills, Pete. I'm an adult now. I've learned to work with all kinds of people, and if someone gets angry, I can either step away or communicate clearly and create boundaries. Not everyone is Sister Mary, screaming if we say the wrong thing."*

Pete: *"So what do I do?"*

You: *"Let's make a new agreement about how to work together. What if, instead of protecting me from people, you stick close by my side? If it feels like there's danger, just tap on my shoulder."*

Pete: *"I could do that."*

Notice that you aren't asking permission of Pete. You're explaining to Pete what **you** want and you're working it out with him.

You're taking your authority and responsibility back into your own hands rather than just letting Pete step in and run the show. You're explaining to Pete how you want things to change and checking in with him—but you call the shots. That's what we mean by restoring authority. We are restoring your authority with your team.

HIJACKED BY BILLY THE KID

Josh was an expert in his field, one of the best business consultants in all of the Silicon Valley. He had years of experience and a strong network of colleagues and friends. His business was good, including several clients who had been with him for years.

At one point, when the economy took a dip, some of his long-term clients tightened their belts and began to cut back on the work they were doing with Josh. It was time for him to go get more clients.

As a business consultant, Josh knew all about creating a marketing plan. He knew exactly what needed to happen, including reaching out to colleagues, making warm calls and cold calls, and generally letting people know what he had to offer and inviting them to work with him.

CHAPTER 5

But every time he went to make calls to expand his business, he thought, "Nobody wants to hear from me. I'll just be bothering them." Without even noticing, he turned his attention away from making calls and found other work to focus on—some e-mail to check, something "more important."

This happened every few days. It went on for weeks, maybe months. Then one day, Josh noticed that he had been hijacked.

So Josh started listening. Who was this? He asked that Player to say more, and this is what he heard: "People are really busy. I want to respect their time. I don't want to interrupt. Respect is important." As he listened, he heard the legitimacy of this point of view; after all, respect was one of Josh's highest values. He allowed himself to "feel his way in" to this Player and noticed how nervous he felt: his stomach and solar plexus felt tied in knots. Kind of like a kid who didn't want to make his father mad.

It was pretty surprising for this successful middle-aged man to realize that a scared little boy was in charge of his sales department!

Once Josh really became aware of this kid, he was able to grab onto that scared, nervous energy and pull it out. He was able to separate from it, sort of like taking off a shirt and holding it at arm's length, so that he could take a look at it. He imagined that little boy out in front of him and started to see a sweet, nervous boy about eight years old. He named him Billy the Kid.

Continuing to do this Inside Team work, Josh realized that somehow he had given Billy the Kid a job assignment that he just wasn't suited for. As a mature adult, Josh knew that he needed another Player, another part of him, to step up and run his sales department.

> *But before he went there, the next step was to get in better relationship with Billy.*
>
> *At some point, many years ago, perhaps without even knowing it, Josh had invited (or perhaps just allowed) Billy the Kid to step in and protect him. Billy got the idea that he had to protect Josh from unknown situations. Billy saw it as a pact: he would step in whenever Josh was about to do anything that might be seen as disrespectful.*

Josh decided to have a conversation with Billy the Kid to find out about their Silent Pact, and it went something like this:

Josh: "Hi there. Is it OK if I call you Billy the Kid?"

Billy: "Sure; I kinda like it."

Josh: "So, I noticed that whenever I go to make phone calls, you say, 'Nobody wants to hear from me. I'll just be bothering them.' What's going on?"

Billy: "If you call and it's the wrong time, they might not like you. It's important that you respect their time. It's important that they respect you."

Josh: "Sounds like respect is really important to you."

Billy: "You bet it is!"

Josh: "What else are you concerned about?"

Billy: "Well, I don't want you to get hurt."

Josh: "Hurt how?"

CHAPTER 5

Billy: *I don't want anyone to yell at you and hurt your feelings. You might not be able to handle it."*

Josh: *"Hmm. Really? When I was little, I did get scared when someone yelled at me. I'm grown up now, and actually, I don't think people are going to yell at me because I call them."*

Billy: *"They might!"*

Josh: *"Well, they might, but I doubt it. I can respectfully ask to set a time to talk with them."*

Billy: *"Huh."*

Josh: *"I really appreciate how you've been taking care of me over the years, but I don't need you to protect me this way anymore, at least not around making calls."*

Billy: *"Oh…." (disappointed).*

Josh: *"What if we gave you another job?"*

Billy: *"Like what?"*

Josh: *"Like, what if you get to go play more? And, if you see that someone is not respecting me, you can whisper in my ear to point it out. You don't have to jump out front and handle it for me; just give me that nudge and I'll take care of it."*

Billy: *(relieved) "OK, I can do that."*

Josh: *"Thanks. Let's try it. If it's not working, we can always talk again."*

TRAPPED IN THE BLANKET

Here is an example of a Player who was hijacking the situation in a feeling/emotional way:

Ron was stuck. He was working on a project that just wasn't moving forward. This was unusual for Ron; he was good at getting things done. But this was different, and he didn't know why. As we started looking at his experience through the lens of his Inside Team, Ron realized that he felt a kind of paralysis surrounding this project. When he tried to pull the feeling out and put it in front, he couldn't. It was as though his arms were pinned down and he was wrapped up in a blanket—almost like a straitjacket. He realized that this project represented a huge life shift, and he was feeling paralyzed by the idea of this change. Once Ron got a sense of this "blanket," I asked if he could take the blanket off. He grabbed onto that blanket feeling and imagined pulling the blanket off. Then he had a conversation with this Player—the Blanket.

As they spoke, he found that the Blanket's job was to nurture him, to keep him safe. But in this instance, the Blanket was keeping him too safe. The Blanket wanted to keep him from failing. Ron talked to the Blanket, letting it know that he didn't need it to keep him from making a mistake or failing anymore. He actually would love if the Blanket could be just that—a blanket that would keep him warm and be there for him during deep emotional times. He asked the Blanket if it would be nurturing and create that trusting, safe space when he needed it. And just like that, the Blanket was no longer smothering him. The Blanket was a comfort instead. And Ron was able to move forward with his project.

CHAPTER 5

BULLYING OR CONSCIOUS CHOICE?

Do you feel safe inside yourself?

When we feel safe in our own skin, inside ourselves, we are amazing. We create, we imagine, we are curious about the world and other people. We try new things and are open to new ideas; we are not afraid.

However, most of us, everyone that I know, has at least one place where it's not entirely safe.

In our society we're often taught that if we can't rule our internal voices, then something is wrong with us. This concept of willpower means that we should suppress our inner voices, some of our Players. But really, what we are doing is bullying ourselves. We berate ourselves for thinking certain things. We say to ourselves, "I can't think that" or "I shouldn't think that" or "I'm so stupid for thinking that way. Why can't I be different?" We beat the crap out of ourselves.

What if instead, we slow down and bring curiosity to the situation? What if we listen to those other Players, even the ones who we don't like so much, and consider what they have to say, what they have to offer? What if there's a bigger picture here that's not just black or white, all or nothing, dominating or permissive?

Ignoring these other voices will make them pop up when you least expect it. Later, you'll find yourself thinking things like, "I hate how I handled that situation. That's not me … I don't even know who that person was!" Surprise! It was a hijacking Player, and until you sit down and chat with them, they'll keep appearing when you least expect it. When you become aware of each of your players and get into a conversation with them (rather than ignoring them or muscling them with willpower), then you get to make conscious choices.

SAFE SEX

The year was 1974. She had been dating Dan, her first love, her high school sweetheart, for over a year. It was clear to her that she would be with him forever—that it was just a matter of time before the two of them would be married.

So it didn't seem like such a big deal for them to lose their virginity to each other. Fumbling around, they weren't great lovers yet, but they had been having fun and enjoying each other.

Then one night, Dan made the mistake of saying, "If you get too fat, I'll never make love to you again."

For eighteen-year-old Sandy, that's all it took. It made no difference that he wasn't really reacting to her—this little cutie pie who weighed about 102 pounds. He was reacting to his mother, a morbidly obese woman who had not seen the lower side of 350 pounds on her scale since before she was pregnant with her last child.

What Sandy heard was that she was too fat—or almost too fat—right now. It was in that moment, with those words, when sex was no longer safe.

From that moment on, every time Sandy was in a romantic situation with a boy, and later with her husband, the voice in her head would run a nonstop monologue that sounded something like this: "He wants to have sex with you, but what if he thinks you're fat? You are fat! He's probably noticing your stomach—hold it in."

Surprisingly, this voice never spoke during a time of flirting or even foreplay. It only started right when actual sex was starting to occur. Sandy would have to stop things because the voice was just too

CHAPTER 5

> *loud. Almost every sexual encounter was unfulfilling and ended in tears.*
>
> *Sandy was about forty-two years old when she finally got her hands on this Player: the Guard. She finally realized that she didn't have to buy the shaming, protecting, hiding game that it was selling. It took lots of patience and love, from her husband and from Sandy herself, but bit by bit she learned to relax and feel safe in her own skin in the bedroom.*

This kind of work takes a great deal of intimacy. It can be as difficult to be intimate with ourselves as with another human being, sometimes more so. It's a vulnerable act to be willing to notice the subtle ways that we belittle and shame ourselves, the stories that we concoct to distance ourselves from others, and the myriad of ways that we uncomfortably and painfully try to keep ourselves safe.

I invite you to slow down and notice the places in your life where you feel bad about yourself. Chances are, there is a Player in there somewhere.

CHAPTER 6

BULLIES AND GANGS

We're all about paying attention to your Players. But what if there's a Player that's just beating you up? What if it's telling you you'll never be good enough, pretty enough, or strong enough? In fact, it tells you that *you* aren't enough?

This isn't a Hijacking Player, nor is it a Triggered Player. This, my friends, is a Bully. Would you tolerate it if someone on the outside bullied you this way? I hope not. I hope you would find a way to interact with or move away from the bully so that they could not continue to dominate you. So how can you take charge of the bully in your head?

Same as always—you need to start a conversation. You need to find out what this Player is trying to get you to hear. So far, the way it's communicating is awful. It makes you want to shut down or say "screw you!" But there's still something here to consider.

Working with a Bully can be particularly challenging. It's an easy way

CHAPTER 6

to get triggered. However, when we can ground ourselves and become curious about this Bully, then we have a chance.

While the *way* this Bully is talking and carrying on might be really nasty, see if you can find a small amount of truth within it. The Bully would have you believe that what it has to say is the **only** truth. However, that is not really the case.

"You are too old for this!" the Bully shouts.

"You are crappy at Sudoku! You are wasting your time!"

*"You'll **never** be able to pull this off!"*

Notice that Bullies often communicate in a dramatic, all-or-nothing tone. That is a part of their power. This drama, this use of absolutes, creates an "amygdala hijack," a phrase that Daniel Goleman coined in his book **Emotional Intelligence**. The power of a Bully or Trigger is that it momentarily throws you back on your heels, wiping out your ability to engage as an adult. Yes, your prefrontal cortex will come back online at some point and you will have that "What just happened?" feeling.

When a Bully shouts at you, trying to make you believe what they say is "the Truth," try listening for the "wisdom aspect" of what it says or the tiny little grain of truth that is hidden inside.

"It's **not safe**!" might become "Let's make sure that you are safe."

"You suck at this!" might become: "Hum, you might need some practice if you want to be good at this."

The steps to working with a Bully are very much like working with a Triggered Player.

HOW TO WORK WITH AN INSIDE TEAM BULLY

Before you go further, get solidly grounded in yourself. Find the mature, strong You who can be curious about the Bully without feeling frightened or belittled. In order to do this piece of work, You cannot be ready to buy what the Bully is selling.

Note: When you think about the Bully, if you have an immediate reaction of fear or nervousness, chances are that is another Player hijacking you. It's normal for child Players to feel afraid of other Players, particularly Bullies. So, if a terrified part of you, or One Who Believes the Bully shows up, go back a few pages and practice restoring authority. Have that scared Player go somewhere safe and let them know that you don't expect them to handle the Bully.

Bring your awareness to the Bully. What does the Bully say to you?

As with other Players, bring the Bully out in front and imagine it. It can be extremely useful to imagine these Players as cartoon figures from a Disney movie rather than characters from *Pulp Fiction, Deliverance,* or *Game of Thrones.*

Notice what the Bully uses to have you feel bad: Comparisons? Guilt? Shame? Blame*? To understand more about the Bully's power and how to work with it, check out the work of John Gottman and what he calls "The Four Horsemen of the Apocalypse."*

Sometimes Bullies will scream questions at you such as, **"What if it doesn't work out?"**

Let's lower the scream down to an indoor voice; let's take the panic and urgency out of it and turn it into a calm question. It's not a bad question.

Ground yourself and take a moment to consider the question. You are creative, resourceful, and whole. If a situation doesn't work out the way you hope it will, I bet that you could figure out a new way forward without much of a problem.

Sometimes these Bullies scream louder and louder because we haven't stopped to listen to and respond to the question.

Sometimes Bullies make loud accusations or declarations:

"You never visit your mother!!! You are a bad daughter!!"

They are used to having you respond in a particular way. Perhaps you sheepishly feel bad, perhaps you internally scream back, "Screw you!," Perhaps you defend yourself, "Well, I've been really busy lately ..."

What they are not used to is you **not** taking the bait. It might sound something like this:

Your Uptight Schoolmarm Bully screams: *"You never visit your mother!!! You are a bad daughter!!"*

You: *"Stop. The way that you are speaking to me right now doesn't work."*

Uptight: *"What? You know I'm right!! You never visit your mother!!!"*

You (calmly): *"There is something that you are trying to offer me here, but I can't tell what it is. You screaming at me like this is not useful."*

At this point, you get to stay calm and curious. What does "You never visit your mother" actually mean? What is it trying to tell you? Let's turn down the volume and the intensity and find the useful information underneath the blame.

First, chances are that it's not entirely accurate to say, "You never visit your mother." Maybe it is more accurate to say "You visit your mother sometimes," or "You would like to spend more time with your mother." What is the more accurate version for you?

Next, look underneath the accusation. What is it pointing to? Do you want to make sure that your mom knows that she is loved? Do you miss connecting with her (as she declines)? Do you wish that you had a stronger relationship with her? Perhaps you need to take a big-picture look at all of your commitments and create a plan or schedule that includes seeing your mom. On the other hand, perhaps you would prefer to stop visiting her, but you're just not clear on how to do that.

In other words, if this were not about visiting your mother, what would it be about?

HIJACKING GANGS

Sometimes Players gang up to bully you. They band together or latch onto one very strong player in order to get on the hijacking bandwagon. Let's take a look at how this happens with gangs.

As we discussed earlier, sometimes your team is working together so well, you don't even know they're there. But sometimes you have a whole group of players who seem to be working against you—not just one player but a few that hang out together. This is a gang.

Certain creative Inside Team Players will create alliances to support each other or to collude about what they want. You may already know these gang members individually. They don't always show up together, but when they do, they pile on to strengthen and amplify each other's voices and positions. They can gang up to support one primary hijacking Player or come two or three at time.

CHAPTER 6

A gang of Players might sound something like this:

Whiny Willy: *"It's too hot to go exercise. I don't want to."*

Overprotecto: *"And it's not good for you to work out in the heat. You might get sick."*

The Fact Master: *"That's right, tests have shown that if you work out in temperatures above 100 degrees, it could cause an electrolyte imbalance."*

Overprotecto: *"Oh, my God. You could die!"*

No wonder you get taken off course.

In this case, the gang is looking for a reason not to work out, and they've found plenty: it's too hot; you're too tired; you have too much work to do. They've even thrown in a death threat! But once you become aware that you're being ganged up on, you can bring in an ally (see Chapter Seven) who will remind you what you want and what you committed to. Keep in mind, sometimes the gang has a point. It really might be too hot for you to work out that day. But when you're on autopilot and not making a conscious choice, the above conversation goes on in your head, and before you know what happened, you're popping open a beer in front of the TV.

When you're aware that there's a hijacking team in action, you get to stop and ask yourself what you're committed to, what you want, and what will work in conjunction with your real desires in the present moment. If it's 100 degrees today, you might decide to work out on Friday instead. But you won't feel bad, because you chose. You didn't just blindly give in to the voices in your head. Or you might decide that you do want to work out—indoors!

If you can identify a gang's ring leader, you rarely have to pull the whole team apart. Everybody will probably fall in line behind him or her. In our workout example, the leader is Overprotecto. Design a new agreement with him, and you can settle the entire gang.

WHEN A TEAM BECOMES A GANG

Here's an example of a team that usually works well for Joanne. But under certain circumstances, this team will hijack her and become a gang.

Joanne loves planning things—trips, galas, dinner parties. She loves dreaming about the event and how it's all going to come together. And she's fabulous at it! Friends come to Joanne for advice on planning a birthday party or their itinerary for their next trip. Nothing makes her happier, and she has an Inside Team of Players who support her at every turn. The Planner gets all the details: Where? When? Who? Next, the Researcher finds every possibility at every price point so that every great choice is on the table. Finally, the Dreamer imagines how all the different possibilities might fit together. This team works beautifully for Joanne, **except** when she's dealing with a human being who doesn't like to plan. In that case, her obsession with planning can create a major struggle. It might be a friend, it might be her husband—all of a sudden, Joanne is hijacked by this great need to share every detail! If the other person's not in the mood, watch out.

Here's what happens for Joanne:

The Planner is pissed off because his hands are tied. The Researcher feels discounted because of all the work she's done. The Dreamer is disappointed that the dream can't come together. Suddenly Joanne's team is a gang, and they're throwing a massive hissy fit:

Planner: *"I'm just trying to get this done and you won't help. Unbelievable!"*

Researcher: *"Don't look at me! I did all this work for nothing!"*

Dreamer: *"I'm surrounded by people with no imagination! We'll never make this trip happen."*

And all Joanne's friend had said was, *"I can't really do this right now."*

THE GOTTA-DO GANG

Henrick had a hijacking gang. He named them the Gotta Do Gang. This gang consisted of Gotta Get It Done, Gotta Do It Right, and Gotta Do It NOW! This gang adopted Henrick's values of action and excellence and took them to a place that didn't feel good for him. The Gotta-Do Gang was willing to do anything and everything to get things done. They didn't care about anyone or anything but the task at hand. Henrick had to pull this gang apart, look at them all separately, and see what they wanted to stand for in his life. Only then could he see where his operating system wasn't working and how he could utilize the Gotta-Do Gang more effectively.

CHAPTER 7

BRINGING IN ALLIES

Now that you know how to work with your Inside Team, you may want to bring in a new Player (or two!) to have your team work more effectively. Most of us have role models in our lives—a favorite teacher, our grandmother, a movie or TV character we identify with, a literary hero. We may bring in their wisdom simply by thinking of them and imagining what they would tell us to do.

What allies could you invite to help reconfigure your Inside Team?

If you are looking to increase your fitness, perhaps you will find your inner Athlete or Ninja Warrior. Want to become a better cook? Why not bring in Julia Child, Bobby Flay, or Masaharu Morimoto? Is it time to do your taxes? Find that Player who is good at math, or perhaps John Deere—like the tractor—the one who knows how to just keep going and will get 'er done.

CHAPTER 7

Your prospects are as wide as your imagination. You can dream up and bring in all kinds of audacious allies—a great character from a movie or book, a person from history who has made an impact on you, or a totally new character you've made up for the job. You can even call in spiritual allies such as God, the Holy Spirit, or Buddha.

In fact, many of us have allies that we already turn to: You are getting ready for a big presentation and you consciously get in touch with the part of you that is confident and knows her stuff. Some people wear a wristband with the letters: WWJD (What Would Jesus Do?) as a way to be reminded of His wisdom.

So bring in Jedi Master, Captain Kirk, Thich Nhat Han, Oprah, or Wonder Woman. Tap into your inner Leader, your inner Nelson Mandela, Gloria Steinem, or Ellen DeGeneres. Look for the person who can shine a light on that awareness—just the image of them will remind you that you want to handle this situation differently.

They could be additional aspects of you, such as your Wiser Self. Or they could represent key people in your external life—your coach, your best friend, even your personal trainer or financial planner.

Many of us naturally look for allies, whether internal or external. How many times have you needed to talk to one special person on the phone when you're going through something because you know they'll help you feel better? **That's** an ally. You can bring that person in as a Player, imagining that person on your Inside Team, so their support is available to you whenever you need it. It becomes a part of you and your consciousness. What do you get from that person? What's the new awareness that their wisdom brings to you?

Remember Julie and her Player, Joan of Arc? Well, Julie already had an ally; she just wasn't utilizing her. Joan of Arc was sitting on her shoulder telling her to go get it—she was strong and smart enough to get where she wanted to go. Before, Julie was letting the others drown Joan out, but now she could really hear her. She could picture Joan of Arc on her horse, ready to take on the world.

The image not only made Julie smile, but it helped her to find her own power and strength. Now that Julie knew whom to call on when she started to hear voices of doubt, she could access Joan so much more easily. Julie was able to bring in Joan of Arc's confidence to start charting her course ahead.

TAKING A TIP FROM BASEBALL'S BEST

Jared played college baseball and was the catcher for his team. He was a senior, and he desperately wanted to look good for scouts. Because of this, Jared was overthinking and overplaying every time he got on the field. He would use all of his energy in the first game of a three-game series. By the time he got to the third game, he didn't have anything left to give. He was tired, he was sloppy, and the whole team suffered.

When Jared started to look at his Inside Team, he found a hijacking Player whom he named Little League. Little League wanted to be the hero, to have all eyes on him. Little League wanted to win the game at any cost—and that meant he had to go after every ball. So he played foolishly. By the middle of the second game, he was spent. He wasn't thinking; he was just reacting so that he could be a part of the action.

Jared was a fan of the legendary baseball player Yogi Berra— one of the greatest catchers of all time. Berra loved being behind the plate, seeing the whole field and knowing the intricacies of the game. He was always a step ahead. He knew what his moves should be before the pitch ever came. In a three-game situation, Berra knew which plays were crucial and required all his energy and which allowed him to hold back and let someone else lead. He was able to pace himself; that's how he could play as well in the third game as in the first.

Jared had always idolized Yogi Berra and wanted to emulate him, but up until this point, he couldn't seem to access him in his games.

As we talked, Jared told Little League that it was time for him to sit on the bench for games. He asked Little League to come on full-force in practice, but to step back and rest for games and let Yogi Berra be in control. Little League didn't have the maturity to know what was needed in the games. But he was perfect for going all-out and trying new things in practice.

The next time Jared played, a different player stepped onto the field. His whole game changed. He made smart moves. He played hard when necessary and stepped back when it didn't really matter. Jared's Inside Team work literally got his head back in the game.

Paradoxically, sometimes the ally you most need is a real live person—someone with skills or personality traits that complement yours or someone who can hold you accountable. By building new relationships or strengthening existing ties with such people, you can accomplish tasks that would be impossible alone. For example, if you're looking to handle your finances, but none of your Inside Team Players know how to work with money, then finding an accountant or taking a financial planning course will likely be more effective than finding your inner tax man—at least initially. Once you have learned the skills you need, then you will have that inner ally to call on.

CHAPTER 8

CREATING A NEW PLAYBOOK

WHO IS IN CHARGE?

It was eye-opening for my client Cheryl when I said, "I want you to imagine that these Players on your Inside Team are your employees and you're the boss."

Cheryl (indignant): "I would never have employees talk to me like that!!"

Coach: "So if you had an employee who did start to talk that way, what would you do?"

Cheryl: "I would let them know that this behavior was unacceptable! I would try to find out what it was that they were being so nasty about. I might give them a new job assignment, but I certainly would not have them *managing people. And I would definitely let them know that it was not OK for them to talk to me that way ever again."*

Coach: *"It sounds like you would step into your authority and set clear boundaries—perhaps create a new way of working with that employee or even take them off that job?"*

Cheryl: *"Yes, exactly."*

Cheryl took home a list of questions to consider:

✏️ EXERCISE 10: DESIGNING THE NEW PLAYBOOK

- When it comes to this topic, how do I want it to go?

- Who are the Players already on my Inside Team for this topic?

- What are they each trying to do?

- What is the truth or wisdom that each one brings?

- What do I appreciate about each one?

- What roles are they playing? Are those the right roles for them?

- When I put them out in front of me, what do I become aware of?

- What is the energy and dynamic of this team?

- Who has been stealing the show?

- Is there any particular player who has been hijacking me?

- Whom have I been automatically believing?

- Whom have I not heard (much) from?

- Where have I been giving up my own authority?

- What does this new information give me?

- If the game were played my way, how would I actually want it to go?

- What are the new agreements that we need to make?

- How do I want this team to operate?

- What can we all align on?

So now that you're back in charge, **you** get to decide how you'd like to work with this team moving forward. You get to talk to your players and make the choices about how each of your players can serve your agenda. You take charge.

It may help to think of it this way: Imagine that all the Players on your Inside Team are like the executive leadership team of a major corporation. Imagine them seated around a huge conference table in the corporate offices.

They each come in with their particular areas of expertise. They each hold unique information that the team needs. They each champion a unique mix of values in service of the corporation, depending on the position they hold. If even one of their voices is not heard and honored, the corporation as a whole will suffer.

Now, in walks the CEO. This is YOU—the core essence of who you are. The CEO calls the meeting to order. She moves it forward with her own agenda. She listens to all the Players around the table. She takes in their advice. She brokers agreements among the Players to help them work together more effectively. But at the end of the day, the ultimate authority to choose where the corporation will go and what it will do rests with the CEO—not the executive team. She makes the final call and assigns Players the roles and tasks that will take the organization where she wants it to go.

In other words, you are facilitating new agreements and a new way for this Inside Team to work together on the project at hand. This alliance-building process looks much like any other partnership you may find in the "outside" world. You listen to all voices, find their common interests and desires, and move them toward agreement to work together in a new and powerful way that works for you.

RUNNING THE NEW PLAY

Joyce had been working with her Inside Team on finances. After noticing that she had constantly been hijacked by her inner eight-year-old, (who was really smart but hated handling money), she went through the steps to restore authority and design a new playbook with her Inside Team. This is what she reported to me the following week:

Arriving home after a hard day, I was disappointed to discover some bills that need to be paid. Automatically, my eight-year-old Player waved her hand and asked, "You want me to get this? I'm happy to freak out!"

Before we started this work, my eight-year-old would have just hijacked me. I would have freaked out, been upset all evening, and never have paid the bills. This time, a smile came to my face. I was aware that she was there and delighted that she was so eager to help. I had a moment then—a split second of choice. In that moment, I thanked her for volunteering and reminded her that handling money is not her job. As an eight-year-old, I want her to go out and play. She liked that reminder.

I remembered the work we had done with my Inside Team, and as I considered which Player could handle this more effectively, I was tapped on the shoulder by an inner ally, a Player that I now call my Calm Leader. She said, "Relax. Everyone has bills to pay. You know how to add and subtract. Let's just sit down, take a look at the numbers, and get this done. You are safe."

Nice work, Joyce!

JULIE PUTS IT ALL TOGETHER

Let's circle back to our friend Julie one more time. When we started all of this she was frustrated, burned out, and feeling hopeless. Over the chapters of this book, we have seen Julie get to know her main Players: Fire Fighter, Penny Saver, Timid Mouse, Wise Owl, and Joan of Arc. She took the time to restore authority with the Fire Fighter, which has helped to shift the dynamic of the team. Leaning in to Joan of Arc, she saw the need for another ally, one that she calls the Researcher.

She sat down with her team and started mapping the new game plan.

Julie: "OK, team. Here's what's going to happen: We have brought in the Researcher. Her job is to find out three things: 1) What is the path for *someone to become a speech pathologist? What training do they need? What credentials? 2) Who offers this training? When do they offer it? And 3) How much does it cost? Are there scholarships or payment plans available? Once we have that information, we can start to make a plan forward. How does that sound?"*

The Team: *(looks at each other, surprised, yet nodding with general consent.)*

Joan of Arc: *"That sounds like a plan. Let's get this party started."*

Julie has some strong Players on her team. They won't always just go along with her; that's not their job. However, now that they have seen that Julie is in fact an adult and knows what she wants, they are ready to align and move forward together.

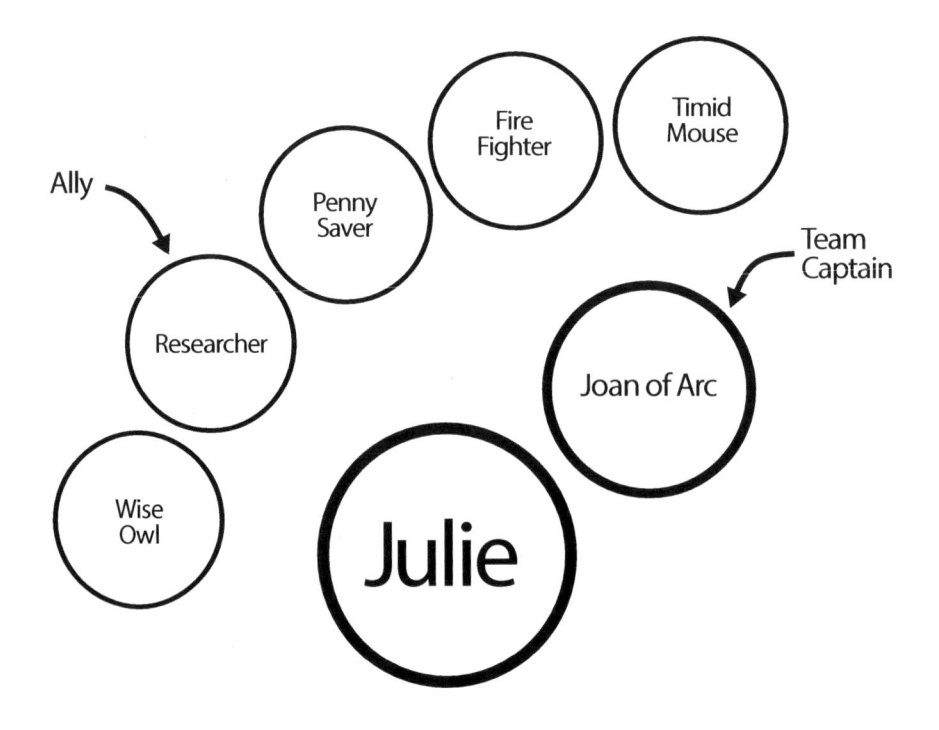

CREATING A NEW PLAYBOOK

BEN'S BOARDROOM

CARING FATHER
- Sees others as God sees them
- Love others as God does

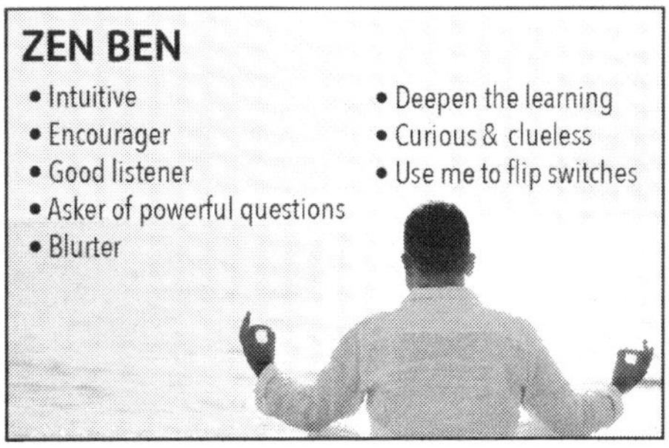

ZEN BEN
- Intuitive
- Encourager
- Good listener
- Asker of powerful questions
- Blurter
- Deepen the learning
- Curious & clueless
- Use me to flip switches

EMBRACE
- Lean in
- Embrace
- Love tenderly
- Looks for "thin places"

SPLAT MAN
- The world is going to end.
- I am going to die.

ANSWER MAN
- Expert
- Consultant
- Sit down, shut up, and listen

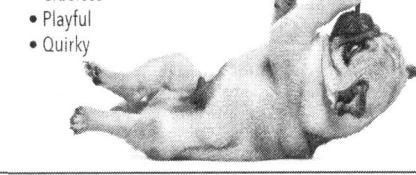

ROSIE THE PUG DOG
- Curious
- Clueless
- Playful
- Quirky

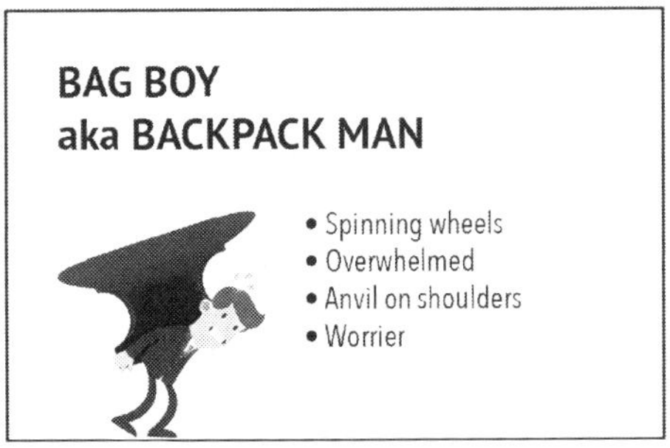

BAG BOY aka BACKPACK MAN
- Spinning wheels
- Overwhelmed
- Anvil on shoulders
- Worrier

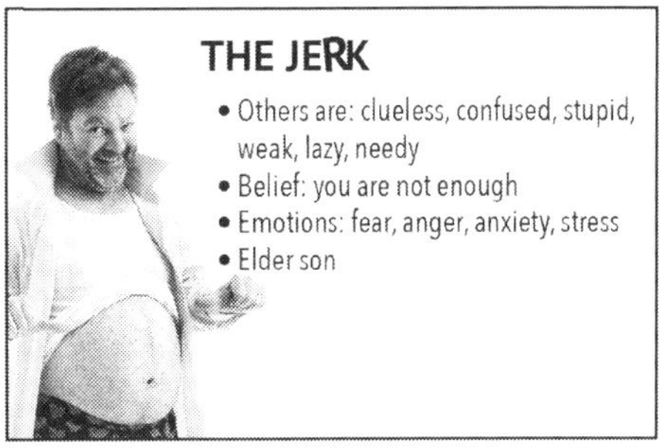

THE JERK
- Others are: clueless, confused, stupid, weak, lazy, needy
- Belief: you are not enough
- Emotions: fear, anger, anxiety, stress
- Elder son

115

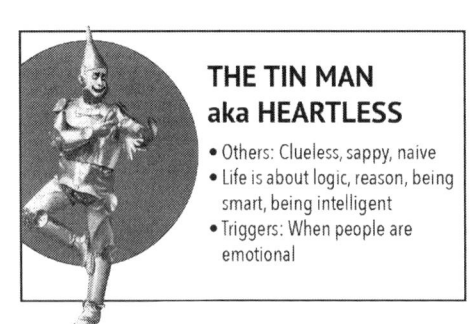

THE TIN MAN aka HEARTLESS
- Others: Clueless, sappy, naive
- Life is about logic, reason, being smart, being intelligent
- Triggers: When people are emotional

PRESENT PERFECT
- Now here (vs Nowhere)
- Quirky pug dog humor
- Laugh MORE – myself and make others laugh
- Abandon, whimsy, love

CALVIN
I am playful, confident, mischevious, ready for action, and MORE than enough!

PURPOSE
Catalyzing & developing emotionally intelligent leaders and their systems to be better, more efficient, more productive, more sustainable, more resilient, and more fulfilling.

As you get to know your Players, there are so many creative ways to be in a relationship with them. Sometimes people make a list or a collage. I got a kick out of this one and asked to share it with you. Ben is one of our Inside Team coaches. He put together his "Boardroom"—his chart of power Players. Looking at the pictures and reading through the bullet points gets him in touch with the energy and wisdom of each of these Players. It reminds him of the smart, powerful, and creative man that he is and grounds him as he starts or ends his day.

CHAPTER 9

MOVING FORWARD

My sincere hope, and the reason that I wrote this book, is for you experience relief from the patterns that have been running you—for you to know a greater sense freedom and personal power. This work has opened up my creativity and given me permission to live life on my terms. It has healed my heart and increased my ability to be compassionate and loving to others. While there is always room to grow, and more to discover about my Players and Inside Teams, this work works. I hope and trust that you have found at least a few of these ideas useful in how you think about yourself and your relationships with your Inside Teams.

In the next pages, you will find all of the questions that we asked throughout the book so that you can use them as a workbook at any time.

"The Inside Team" was first created in 2006 by Cynthia Loy Darst and her team as a training for advanced professional coaches. If you would like to learn more about Inside Team coaching, reach out to Cynthia Loy Darst at **Cynthia@teamdarst.com**.

EXERCISES

EXERCISE 1
QUESTIONS TO HELP YOU DISCOVER YOUR INSIDE TEAM

So take a moment now, and listen in. Think about that project you are working on or thing that you want to change. Notice your thoughts, notice the dialogue, notice your concerns, and take some notes.

Here are a few questions to play with:

- What is the topic—the project or thing you are thinking about?

- What is your first thought about it?

- What other thoughts, concerns, or feelings come in next?

- What else?

- Does it seem like there is a conversation going on?

- What feels familiar?

- What are the different thoughts, energies, or points of view?

EXERCISE 2
IDENTIFY THE PLAYERS

Think of a topic, maybe one from the list above, or the challenge you worked on earlier in the chapter—the situation you'd like to change but can't seem to budge. Take a few minutes to bring that issue to mind. Tune in to the conversation in your head. Notice the thoughts that occur and then start to slow them down.

There's probably a voice that's quite loud, so let's start with that one. Separate it from the others and bring your awareness to it. What is that voice saying? In what tone?

You get to use your imagination here: bring this voice out in front of you and imagine it standing there. What does this Player look like?

- Let yourself imagine it like a character.
- What does it look like?
- How does it stand, sit, or move?
- What gestures does it make?
- How is it dressed?
- How old is it?
- What else do you become aware of?
- It has been working hard to get your attention. What is it trying to tell you?

Repeat these steps with any other Players that come up.

As you start to become more aware of these Players, what are you finding out?

EXERCISE 3
SPOT THE PLAYERS

Here's an example from Becky:

"I'm trying to start this new business, and every time I go to work on my website, there's a part of me that says, "You don't know what you're doing!" I've gone to school, I have my degree, and when I work with a client, not only do I enjoy the work; my clients appreciate me as well. But I just **can't get this voice to go away.**"

So far we have two Inside Team Players. Can you spot them? There are two main points of view being expressed.

Player 1 exclaims: "You don't know what you're doing!"

Player 2 defends: "Yes, you do know what you're doing! You're educated you have clients, and you're enjoying your work."

Dilemma! Conflict! Daytime television in your very own brain! It sounds like these Players are both trying to be right (like there is a **right**), and if we can figure out which one is right, then it will all be settled! However, that's not the way it works. We need more information. We need to know about these Players and what they're playing for. So here's what we did with Becky:

We had Becky put her Players out in front and start to name them. As she did, we discovered a third one who was saying that she needed to hurry up, that she was behind and taking too long with the website.

We came up with a simple chart that looked something like this:

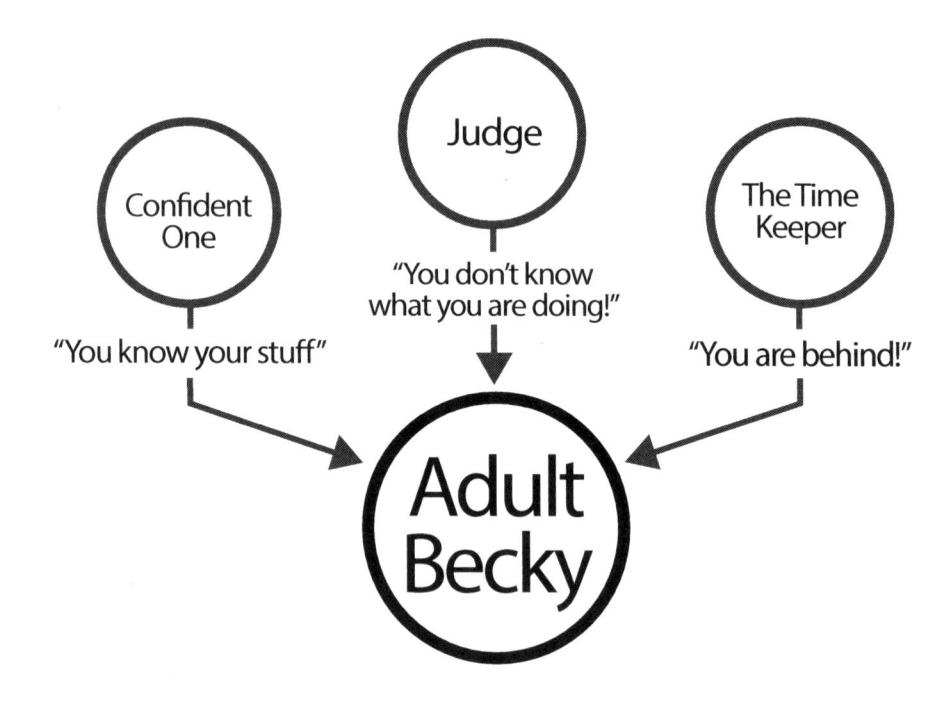

```
        Confident          Judge         The Time
          One                              Keeper

                     "You don't know
                     what you are doing!"
    "You know your stuff"                "You are behind!"

                        Adult
                        Becky
```

Are you starting to get the idea? Now go back to the conversation in your head and begin to chart it out, the way Becky did. You may find you only have two players to start—or you may find five, six, or seven. No matter how many players you discover this time around, chances are you'll uncover more as we move forward.

WORKSHEETS/DIAGRAMS FOR INSIDE TEAM

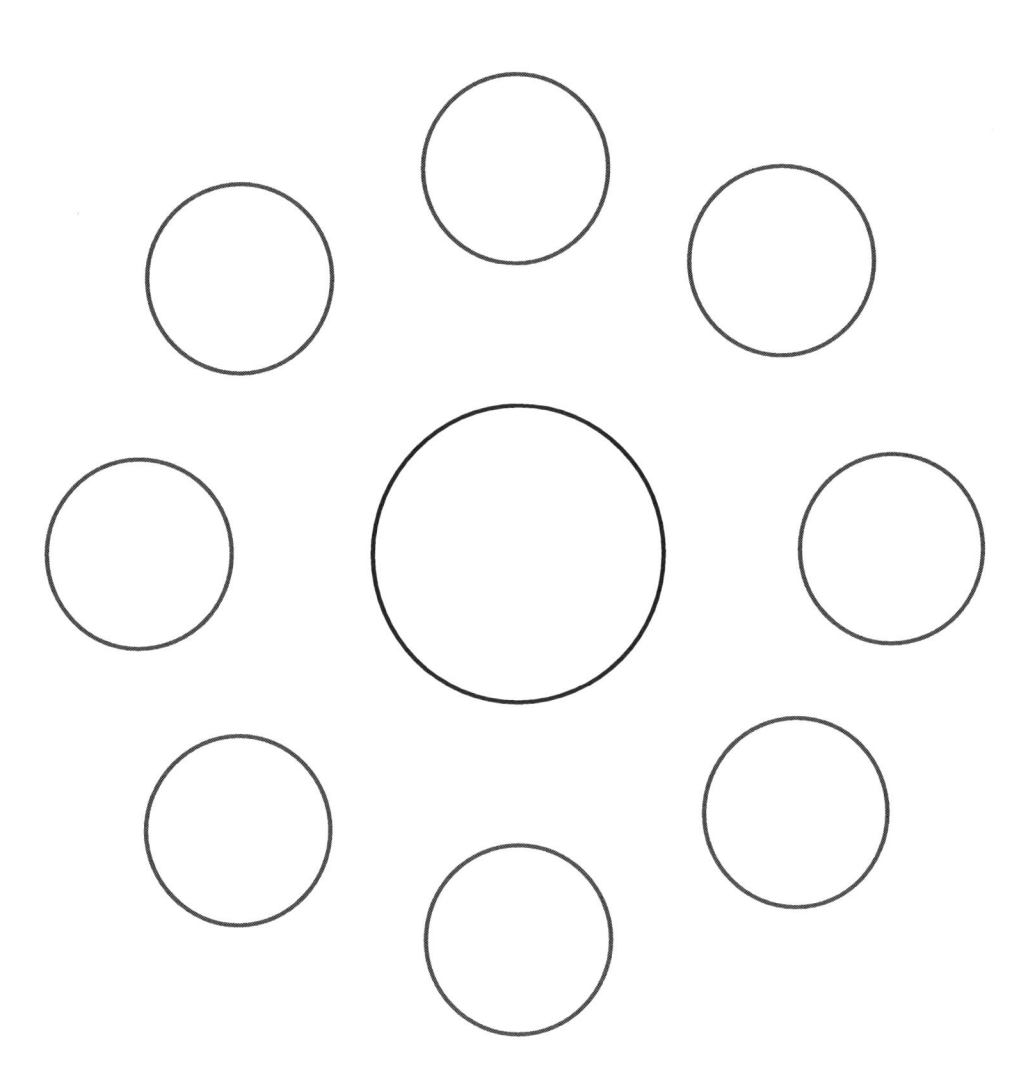

EXERCISE 4
MEET YOUR INSIDE TEAM

You are starting to get the idea of the Players. Now it's time to get them out in front of you so that you can see who you have on the team.

Let's imagine that you are putting them out in front of you, perhaps onto a stage.

At this point, let's just bring them out one at a time and find out more about them.

As you answer these questions, you may want to take some notes:

- Which Player wants to come out first?

- What does the Player look like? Stand/sit like?

- What's important to this Player?

- What is it concerned about?

- What does this Player think you are going to forget?

- What does this Player think its job is?

- What job do they want?

- What do they need from you?

- Does the Player have a relationship with or talk to other players on your team or only with you?

EXERCISE 5
NAMING YOUR PLAYERS

As you start name your players, find names that you relate to, names that will help you personify these players and be able to picture them. For example, I have a player that I call Ms. Train: she's smart, savvy, and impeccably well dressed. She's also a steamroller and quite nasty at times. She will run people over like a train. She is extremely competitive and driven by status.

There are lots of ways to name Players. The one thing that I recommend *against* is naming a Player an emotion.

For example, lets imagine that there is part of you that feels nervous or afraid. If we initially call her Nervous Nelly, then she has some room to shift. As you get to know her, she might calm down and then you can call her Nelly. However, if you start by calling her Fear, then she has nowhere to go.

As you get to know your Players they will become more dimensional. Your Fierce Warrior might be pissed and aggressive today, but he won't always be that angry. As you hear him and get to know what he's trying so hard to do, chances are that he will calm down. Oh, he will still be your Fierce Warrior whom you can call on in a moment's notice. He just won't be pissed off all of the time.

It's perfectly fine to call a Player "The One Who _____." The One Who Stands for Truth, The One with the Open Heart, The One Who Plays by the Rules. One of my favorites was The One Who Will Not Be Named.

Let yourself really picture each Player, one at a time. What are their main qualities? How would you describe them? What values of yours are they waving a flag for? Try on a name. You can always change it later if it's not quite right.

EXERCISE 6
TEAM DYNAMIC

Using your list or the chart you've created for your players, let's start to get a sense of how the team actually operates:

As you asked them to come out in front of you a few moments ago, you may have already gotten a glimpse into this step. Ask your Players once again to come out in front of you. Bring them out one at a time, imagining them out in front of you on a stage:

- Who steps out first? Where does that one go (center stage? Up right?)

- Which one is next?

- And the one after that? (continue to have them come on to the stage—unless they insist on going somewhere else)

- What starts to happen when they are all there?

- How do these Players interact with each other?

- What patterns consistently arise when you think of your topic or goal?

- Do these players communicate to each other? Or do they only speak directly to you? In either situation, what are they saying or doing?

- Who is standing next to whom?

- Which Players are conflict with each other?

- Which Player seems to have the most power?

- Who else is here that you have not heard from?

- What else do you notice?

EXERCISE 7
DISCOVERING YOU

By now, the idea of noticing a Player and putting them out in front of you is starting to feel more familiar.

This time, as you do that, pause to notice that there is **someone** who can see the other Players. That is YOU.

When we were children and we watched movies, we were terrified of the Wicked Witch, the nasty teacher, and the evil characters. We thought that they were going to get us!

As you have grown up, you might still get nervous watching a movie from time to time. However, I assert that generally speaking, you understand that for the story to be compelling there are a variety of roles that need to be occupied. If there is going to be a good guy, there needs to be a bad guy. It makes a story even more interesting when every character has something that they are passionate about, something that they are totally committed to, something that makes them three-dimensional.

Our Inside Teams offer us a rich and wonderful story when we take the time to slow it down, get to know our Players, and stop resisting what they have to offer.

As you rest into the You of you, allow yourself to be curious about and fascinated by your Players. Let yourself explore what is important to them, what they are passionate about, and what they are working so hard to try to get you to see.

In my experience, Players can often come off as nasty, negative, or evil when they don't know how else to get our attention.

As you see the dynamic and the roles that your Inside Team Players have been cast in, you'll also start to see what might work better for your team. When you can get that view of your internal system, you will naturally start to redesign how the game is played.

EXERCISE 8
WHAT TRIGGERS YOU?

Now that you have had a couple of examples, let's turn our attention back to you:

- What kinds of situations trigger you?

- What kinds of people?

- What specifically do they say or do that triggers you?

- How do you know that you are triggered?

- What are your behaviors? Do you freak out? Freeze up? Act superior?

EXERCISE 9
RESTORING AUTHORITY

Notice and Separate

Notice that there is a Player who hijacks you or the one who reacts to the trigger. Usually, you can feel it in your body. Grab on to that energy with your hands and pull it outside of yourself so that you can separate from it and have a conversation.

You might want to work with a partner or a coach to do this—sometimes it can be hard to separate from the Hijacking or Triggered Player.

Describe the Player and Name It

Really personify him or her—what does this Player look like? Sound like? What does their energy feel like? What might you call this Player?

Give Voice to the Player

What is this Player trying to do? What does he want? This Player takes over because he has an important and valid concern. What is this hijacking Player so concerned about? What is the wisdom this Player might have for you?

Find the Unconscious Agreement

Some time ago, you might have been a child, this Player appeared when you needed them. He/she helped you out of a tight spot when the younger you didn't know how to deal with the situation. At that moment, you made an agreement. It's probably an agreement that you don't remember making, that's why we call it the unconscious agreement. What is it that you and this Player agreed to? Under what circumstances is he/she supposed to step in and take over?

Facilitate a Conversation with the Player

In this situation, it's common to ignore the Player or even pretend that he/she doesn't exist. Maybe you've hated that part of yourself, so you've tried to get rid of it. Now it's time to acknowledge this Player and ask why they keep trying to take over. If he/she were a close friend or colleague and you needed to work through a conflict together, what would you say? It's important that your hijacking Player feels fully heard and understood. If they can see that someone else, you or perhaps a different Player, can handle the situation, they might be willing to step down.

Create Clarity

Identify how you want to respond to the situation, instead of having the Player take over.

Create a New Agreement

It's time now to create a new agreement with the Player. While they need to be able to align with it, you need to step into your authority, your adult self, and design the way that you want to respond when that trigger show up again.

Imagine the Trigger (or Hijacking Situation)

Play it out in your mind. How will you enact this new agreement next time this situation occurs?

EXERCISE 10
DESIGNING THE NEW PLAYBOOK

- When it comes to this topic, how do I want it to go?

- Who are the Players already on my Inside Team for this topic?

- What are they each trying to do?

- What is the truth or wisdom that each one brings?

- What do I appreciate about each one?

- What roles are they playing? Are those the right roles for them?

- When I put them out in front of me, what do I become aware of?

- What is the energy and dynamic of this team?

- Who has been stealing the show?

- Is there any particular player who has been hijacking me?

- Whom have I been automatically believing?

- Whom have I not heard (much) from?

- Where have I been giving up my own authority?

- What does this new information give me?

- If the game were played my way, how would I actually want it to go?

- What are the new agreements that we need to make?

- How do I want this team to operate?

- What can we all align on?

WHAT MAKES THE INSIDE TEAM METHODOLOGY UNIQUE?

This idea that there are different parts of us is not a new one; it is as old as the hills. There are references to parts of oneself in many old texts, including the Bible. Over the past hundred years or so, many different ways to explore and work with these voices, also known as subpersonalities, have been created. There is Jungian chair work, transactional analysis, NLP, Voice Dialogue, Internal Family Systems, Lucid Living, Gestalt, and probably many others.

The Inside Team approach sometimes borrows from, sometimes differs from, and sometimes builds on these beautiful methods. If you want to know more about any of these different approaches, check out John Rowan's book *Subpersonalities*, or just Google them.

There are two main distinctions that set this work apart from other kinds of subpersonality work:

1. The Inside Team was created from a coaching stance.

2. Once we have discovered these Inside Team Players, we do Relationship Systems Coaching with them. RSC comes to us from CRRGlobal.com (The Center for Right Relationship)

Let's take those one at a time:
What does it mean to do subpersonality work from a coaching stance? As compared to what? Well, as compared to therapy or counseling. Voice dialogue and some of the others were originally (and mainly still are) therapeutic approaches where the therapist interacts more directly with the parts and asks for certain parts to step forward.

"From a coaching stance" specifically points to Co-Active Coaching, as taught at CTI, The Coaches Training Institute. It means that as we do this work together, we come from the perspective that you, as you explore your Inside Team, are naturally creative, resourceful, and whole. That every part of you, every Player that you come across, has a useful voice to add. In this exploration, we get to be exquisitely curious together. We will offer you questions to support your exploration, but where you go and what you do with your Players is your choice.

I bring all of this up because at first blush The Inside Team may seem similar to the work I have just mentioned. As you get your hands on it, you will notice what makes it distinct. In fact, the most direct connection is to the work of Marita Fridjhon and Faith Fuller at CRR Global. If you have done their Systems Geography course, you will find what inspired this work. You will notice that Inside Team Players might also be known as Secret Selves, and the piece on restoring authority that we will do here is quite similar to de-triggering. After training with (and leading courses for) Marita and Faith for the past several years, I still see myself primarily as a one-on-one coach. So, it was a natural evolution for me to apply their amazing relationship coaching ideas back to my clients. Out of that, The Inside Team approach was born. It is with extreme gratitude that I have received their blessing to develop and teach The Inside Team work.

For more about coaching, check out the Core Competencies of the International Coach Federation (Coachfederation.org), the Co-Active Coaching Model created by CTI (thecoaches.com), and the Organization and Relationship Systems Coaching (ORSC) created by CRRGlobal (CRRGlobal.com), known for their work in relationship, partnership, and team coaching.

HOW THE INSIDE TEAM WAS CREATED

And now, a little background on The Inside Team, where it came from, and the people who have been instrumental in its development:

In 1980, I started the graduate acting program at The University of California, San Diego. The focus of the first year was finding your character from the inside out. My professor, Arthur Wagner, had us apply Eric Berne's transactional analysis work: I'm OK—You're OK (by Thomas Anthony Harris) and Games People Play (by Berne) to script analysis and character development for our work as actors. Wow! I was immediately hooked. So, long before I had heard of coaching, or even personal development, I was exploring the characters in the scenes and plays that we were doing through the lenses of their Parent, Adult, and Child ego states.

While I went on to be a professional actor in New York for a few years, my path took me to Actor's Information Project (AIP) from 1983-89, where I met some of my early mentors including Jay Perry and Henry House (now Henry Kimsey-House). As the years played out, I moved from acting into the newly emerging profession of coaching. When Henry House and his new partners, Laura Whitworth and Karen (soon to be) Kimsey-House, started The Coaches Training Institute by 1992, I was in. I got certified in their program and by 1995 was one of their first two trainers. I have been on their faculty ever since.

In 1997, after I had been coaching a while, Jeanine Mancusi introduced me to the Voice Dialogue work created by Drs. Hal and Sidra Stone. I worked with Brooks Newton as my Voice Dialogue coach for a few months and quickly attained an abundance of new self-knowledge.

In the early 2000's Marita Fridjhon and Faith Fuller came into my life with the brilliant work of CRR Global, then known as The Center for Right Relationship. Their work offered me a whole new context for finding, exploring, and doing relationship coaching with these inner parts.

Chuck Allen, Beth Shapiro, Nicki Weiss, and Michael Warden are the courageous coaching colleagues who, beginning in 2006, helped me develop and shape this work. Wendy Balman, Laura Overstreet Biering, Shannon Bruce, Martha Carnahan, and Rob Seidenspinner have all played an instrumental role in the growth and development of the Inside Team training and in many of the ideas on these pages.

ACKNOWLEDGEMENTS

To have this book come into being took loving support of many: Michelle Pollack, who first put my thoughts to paper; Anne Stockwell, who helped to shape it; Dan Weil, my constant champion and graphics guy; and Howard VanEs and his team at Let's Write Books, Inc., who guided me through the publishing and book cover design processes. Many of the stories in the book, while the names have been changed, come from experiences of my own clients and of the coaching team above, as well as those of Inside Team coaches Drew Lawson, Sara Smith, and Vicky Jo Varner. Alberto Polloni, Antony Parry, Robert Koch, and Lori Shwebke have all added to the process.

My friends Shauna and Demore Barnes, Ann Betz, Amy Kaplan, Chuck Lioi, Tiza Wynn Riley, Sabrina Roblin, Barb Tiber, Catherine Perry, and Rick Tamlyn all cheered me along the way. And, of course, my steadfast powerhouse of a husband, David Darst—he never did care if I finished it, yet he supported every step.

Printed in Great Britain
by Amazon